CYBER SPACES/SOCIAL SPACES

CYBER SPACES/ SOCIAL SPACES

❏ ❏ ❏

CULTURE CLASH IN COMPUTERIZED CLASSROOMS

Ivor Goodson, Michele Knobel,
Colin Lankshear, and J. Marshall Mangan

First published by PALGRAVE MACMILLAN™ in 2002
175 Fifth Avenue, New York, N.Y. 10010 and
Houndmills, Basingstoke, Hampshire, England RG21 6XS.
Companies and representatives throughout the world.

PALGRAVE MACMILLAN is the global academic imprint of the
Palgrave Macmillan division of St. Martin's Press, LLC and of Palgrave
Macmillan Ltd. Macmillan® is a registered trademark in the United States,
United Kingdom and other countries. Palgrave is a registered trademark in
the European Union and other countries.

ISBN 1–4039–6030–5 (paperback) 0–312–21894–X (hardcover)

Library of Congress Cataloging-in-Publication Data
Cyber spaces/social spaces : culture clash in computerized classrooms / by
Ivor F. Goodson . . . [et al.].
    p.   cm.
    Includes bibliographical references (p.) and index.
    ISBN 0–312–21894–X
    1. Educational technology—Social aspects.   I. Goodson, Ivor.

LB1028.3.C93 2002
371.33'4—dc21   2002017057

A CIP catalogue record for this book is available from the British Library.

Design by Letra Libre, Inc.

First edition: December 2002.
10 9 8 7 6 5 4 3 2 1

Printed in the United States of America.

To Malcolm W. Clarkson,
a publisher with purpose and passion.

CONTENTS

ACKNOWLEDGMENTS

As perhaps is fitting given the topics of this work, the manuscript was assembled largely through the use of computer and telecommunications technologies by four people based in four different countries: England, Mexico, the United States, and Canada. Many people assisted in this process in different ways and in different places. The authors offer their gratitude to the following people and institutions for their contributions.

Ivor wishes to thank his colleagues at the University of East Anglia, a supportive conversational community. He also would like to thank Nicky Skivington for her assistance in preparing this manuscript, and as always, his family, Mary and Andrew.

Colin and Michele wish to thank their friends and colleagues in Mexico and Australia who have supported in important ways the research effort involved in producing this book and related work that it draws upon. In particular, we want to thank Angela Guzmán Ruíz, Hilario Rivera Rodríguez, Adolfo Gomez Cortes, Silvia Mendoza Galoz, Rigoberto Morales Landa, Jorge Manuel Sierra Ayil, María Marcela González Arenas, Manuel Medina Carballo, J. Guadalupe Duarte Ramírez, Fausto César Giron Montoya, Enrique Alonso Sánchez Manchinelly, María-Esther Aguirre, Alicia de Alba, Ángel Díaz Barriga, Chris Bigum, Leonie Rowan, Neil Anderson, Ludmila Doneman, Michael Doneman, Bob Bleicher, and participants at Malveny and Yanga Headlands schools. We also gratefully acknowledge economic support from Language Australia, and invaluable institutional support from the Consejo Nacional de Ciencia y Technología, Mexico (CONACyT), the Posgrado en Pedagogía (UNAM), the Centro de Estudios sobre la Universidad/CESU (UNAM), the Faculty of Education and Creative Arts at Central Queensland University, and the School of Education at the University of Ballarat.

Marshall would like to thank the participants in The Watershed Information System project who generously cooperated in his research. That research was supported in part by a proposal-development grant from the Social Sciences and Humanities Research Council of Canada, and by the Office of the Dean of the Faculty of Education, The University of Western Ontario.

ILLUSTRATIONS

TABLES

1

CYBER SPACES/SOCIAL SPACES

As WE ENTER THE TWENTY-FIRST CENTURY, the familiar spaces of formal education are increasingly being invaded and transformed by new information and communication technologies (ICTs). The formerly well-delimited social spaces of classrooms and schools are rapidly being incorporated into the cyber spaces associated with computer programs, word processing, the internet, and the World Wide Web. This book represents an attempt to come to terms with this transformation as something more than a technological change. We will examine it here as primarily a social and cultural phenomenon.

In the Anglo-American countries of the first world, various kinds of technology have always played an important part in shaping the character of education. Over the past two decades, this trend has accelerated and escalated, especially as ICTs have increasingly been introduced. Beginning in the early 1980s, as microcomputers became more affordable, specialized curriculum subjects such as science, mathematics, and computer studies embraced these technologies and began to re-orient their curricula to accommodate them. Especially at the high school level (and particularly within private schools), ICTs have come to have great symbolic value. The imposition—for that is what it has been—of the new technologies on the whole spectrum of classroom-based curricular learning is now almost universal in the developed world, and the trend is ubiquitous across all subjects and levels.

Not surprisingly, this dramatic change has attracted considerable attention from educational researchers. Educational computing has begun to establish itself as a new discipline, with its own professional associations, university departments, and academic journals. While the research conducted within this new discipline continues to examine its implications from "the inside," we think it is important to also maintain a critical perspective that is at least partly on "the outside"—to constantly examine and re-examine the social and cultural implications of educational technologies.

This book is the result of a decade of sustained "watching" and thinking about ICT adoption and practice in schools. Our focus, in this chapter and throughout the book, conceptualizes the new *learning technologies* as a kind of *social technology*. The questions that arise from this perspective center on what happens when a new social technology, like ICT, is imposed on an existing, well-established, and centrally important social technology—the institutions and cultures of schools and schooling.

Learning Technologies and Social Technologies

The new discipline of educational computing has produced a considerable literature reporting individual instances of integrating new ICTs into classroom learning. The majority of this literature, however, focuses on assessing the success of the adoption of computers, in terms of more-or-less immediate, context-specific, teaching and learning objectives. Another significant portion of the literature is given over to discussing the results of studies conducted at state and national levels, which concentrate on documenting what is being done with new ICTs in classrooms. Many of these studies have been commissioned by government education departments or national associations. Their goals have usually been to assess the current state of the art and/or to provide an empirical base for the development of policy, teacher training, and curriculum. The results of such studies have also frequently provided grounds for exhorting or encouraging teachers to emulate exemplary models of practice (see, for instance, OTA 1995; Winters 1996; AAUW 2000).

On the whole, most of these investigations have produced results that are largely inconclusive, or that consist primarily of lists of recommendations with only local and technical import (Bangert-Drowns, Kulik, and Kulik 1985; Becker and Hativa 1994; Liao 1992). Studies that attempted a wider scope often resorted to optimistic crystal gazing, which extrapolated far beyond the classroom data (e.g., Bork 1985; Knapp and Glenn 1996). Knowingly or not, such studies fit in with a long tradition of "techno-utopianism" and optimistic predictions for the technological reform of education (see Dublin 1989; Perelman 1992; Lebaron and Collier 2001).

Of course, there were also a few dissident voices, notably Theodore Roszak (1986) and Douglas Noble (1991), who saw dangers inherent in the technologization of education: the degradation of traditional literacies, for instance, or the overwhelming of alternative modes of education by an instrumentalist model derived from military training. However, such voices were usually drowned out by excited predictions about enhanced academic achievement and the like, thanks to the introduction of digital technologies in classrooms.

Despite these limitations, we should not be too critical of past research when we enjoy the benefits of hindsight. The sorts of questions taken up during the early years of educational computing were reasonable because the educational uses of ICTs were still largely in their infancy. The availability of hardware and software was much more limited than it is today, and the prices were such that only a few schools could afford serious technology applications at all. And there was some research, such as that which we undertook in Ontario in the early 1990s (e.g., Goodson and Mangan 1991a; 1991b; 1992; Goodson, Mangan, and Rhea 1991), that attempted to assess the impact computers were having on classroom and subject cultures, and on teaching and learning styles.

Today, however, it must be acknowledged that research into the influence of educational technology has become much more complex. The influences of ICTs were easier to address when there were fewer computers and fewer kinds of computers; fewer variations in software and its classroom applications; and fewer variables to consider when assessing the effects on curriculum and pedagogy. Not only have computers now become commonplace in the schools of developed countries, they have come to occupy a prominent place in many homes and in the lives of many students, at least among those who can afford them. The "digital divide" (Bolt and Crawford 2000), the separation between those who have regular access to computing and those who do not, has superseded (at least in the public imagination) many of the previous "gaps" between classes, genders, and generations (although it also overlaps and reinforces many of those gaps and often trades in an impoverished conception of "access").

Thus the context of educational computing has changed markedly in the last 20 years. But it is not only the technological environment that has changed—the analytical environment has changed at the same time. The "postmodern turn" has altered the intellectual landscape, and a widespread "suspicion toward metanarratives" has arisen in academia and far beyond (see Lyotard 1984). As a result, the kinds of questions and answers that many educational researchers deal with have been altered in profound ways. Greater attention is being paid to the power relations and ideological forms that underlie important cultural phenomena. And, where questions formulated in terms of "either/or" once dominated intellectual discourse during the era of modernity, there is now a greater tendency to see many cultural phenomena as "both/and."

As is perhaps appropriate to a fundamental icon of postmodernity, analyses of the educational use of computers have begun to take on a more postmodern character. Post-structuralist and discursive analyses of ICT use in education have begun to appear (Rose 2000; Dyer-Witheford 1999). There is a new recognition that the use of ICTs is part of a larger cultural shift that is becoming an increasingly complex and multi-faceted process—a process in which patterns of globalizing domination collide with new opportunities for individual self-expression. Within education, pernicious trends toward privatization, commercialization, standardization, and de-skilling can be seen to coexist with exciting new potentials for previously unavailable educational opportunities (Cummins and Sayers 1995; Lankshear, Peters, and Knobel 1996).

Thus, both the phenomena under study, and the lenses through which we study them, have become more complex and sophisticated since the early 1980s. The older, simpler questions of educational-technology research have been superseded by more complex and subtle questions: What effects are ICTs having upon established cultures of teaching and learning? What happens when a new information technology is inserted into an existing social technology like a school? Do globalizing information technologies promote particular ideological and social forms, or are they sufficiently open to permit varieties of use and incorporation—or both and more, under different conditions? What impact has the ascendancy of personal identity politics had on understanding technology-related educational change?

In order to begin answering these questions, educational research must deepen its exploration and evaluation of alternative forms of technology-rich instruction, and the contexts in which they are situated (Haughey 2000). We must recognize that many of the more didactic forms of computerized instruction that have been assessed to date have not shown strong results, either in terms of their return on the public investment or in initiating new and more rewarding forms of educational experience. But we must not lose sight of the fact that there are still some exciting experiments taking place in the use of computers—experiments that encourage students to explore the world outside the classroom and that expose them to unfamiliar cultures and ideas (Cummins and Sayers 1995; Mangan 1998). In assessing these innovative applications, attention to the quality, content, and use of the resources, and to their unique character, is crucial to understanding them (Knapp and Glenn 1996; Lankshear, Peters, and Knobel 1996). We should also remember that educational technologies may share some similarities with other educational innovations and may face many of the same institutional challenges as they are incorporated into our educational systems.

School as a Social Technology and Space of Sedimented Values and Practices

This book, distinctively among extant works, aims to present a diverse range of cases based on research in three different regions of the Anglo-American "developed" world, conducted during a ten-year period. We hope that, collectively, these cases will offer a rich perspective on the question of what happens when a new social technology is imposed on the established social technology of the school.

The nature and role of school as a social technology has become a common observation in the wake of Michel Foucault's work on techniques and technologies of regulation, surveillance, and discursive formation throughout modernity (Foucault 1980). Grosvenor, Lawn, and Rousmaniere (2000), for example, speak of education in the modern city as being "shaped and regularized" by a means of technology—principally, the technology of the school—comprised of "a complex set of artifacts, actors and structures" together with a set of "socially constructed principles, procedures and processes" (ibid.). This technology was devised to "function efficiently" as well as to realize the specific purpose of social control (ibid.). Grosvenor et al. also speak of the school as a space of confinement that shares "a common architectural language" with other modernist institutions like the prison and the asylum. Thus the theme of regulated spaces can be seen to be central to both Foucault's original conception of social technologies, and to the expansion of that conception in more recent work. Both literally and metaphorically, the establishment and enforcement of boundaries, the enclosure and regulation of physical and ideological spaces, has come to be seen as a key to power relations in a knowledge-based society (Foucault 1980, pp. 259–265).

Steven Hodas (1993) carries the concept of school as a social technology a little further. He identifies schools as "a way of knowing applied to a specific goal," which is one widely accepted definition of "technology." The goal in question, according to Hodas, is to preserve and transmit information and authority, and to inculcate certain values and practices at the expense of others. Hodas describes technologies as being "set(s) of practices glued together by values." The school, he says, is founded on four key institutional and organizational values. These are "respect for hierarchy," "competitive individualization," "receptivity to being ranked and judged," and "division of the world of knowledge into discrete units and categories susceptible to mastery." Over the 150 or more years since the inception of mass compulsory schooling in modern Anglo-American countries, the school has remained "essentially unchanged" in form, and has been dedicated to transmitting "a fairly stable subset" of "all possible knowledge . . . [and] the . . . range of human experience" (1993, p. 2).

Other conceptions of technology provide complementary understandings of school as a social technology. According to the conception made popular and influential by Daniel Bell (1973), a technology is a way of doing things in a reproducible manner. This privileges the implementation or application aspect of technology, whereas the concept preferred by

Hodas emphasizes the conceptual or epistemological aspect of technology. Either way, however, we end up in a similar position with respect to school as a social technology. If we pick up Bell's position, we must ask what it is that schools enable us to do socially in a reproducible manner. The answer might include the sorts of purposes or goals identified by Hodas, or the social control function mentioned by Grosvenor and colleagues.

We may want to think more generally of schools as a way of producing human subjectivities—or particular aspects of human subjectivity—in a reproducible manner. In the literature we find considerable overlap as well as considerable disagreement over what aspects of subjectivity school is supposed to produce and/or reinforce. Those aspects around which wide agreement can be found include dispositions toward experiencing time as compartmentalized and "chunked"; valuing propositional knowledge (knowing that) over procedural or performative knowledge (knowing how to); accepting unequal distributions of goods and differential outcomes of personal or group effort as normal and legitimate; seeing hierarchical social relations as natural; a willingness to defer to expertise; accepting and complying with institutionalized authority; and so on.

Features such as these reveal schools to be social technologies: socially constructed mechanisms intended to produce and reproduce positions from which one can understand the world, in ways that are controlled, categorized, proposed, unequally distributed, and so on. An important corollary of recognizing school as a social technology is to see it also as an institution—a social organism with its own needs for self-preservation, growth, reproduction, and change. As the school has evolved over the past century, it has become an institutional site of sedimented values and practices. As Grosvenor et al. remind us, schools were created as "an intervention in culture and in social production," involving a complex "mix" of such things as "designed purposes, social networks, technical operations, technological innovation and craft skills" (ibid.).

However, the process of what schools become is much more complex. To recognize some of the features of this process as enduring is not to say that they are beyond challenge. As one of the central institutions of social control and indoctrination, schools embody many profound contradictions, and those contradictions serve to open up spaces for both innovation and resistance.

The contradictions of schooling do not grow simply out of organizational frictions, but out of the genuine social conflicts reflected in the competing purposes and functions of educational institutions (Labaree 1997). As a result, each educational innovation comes to represent a new arena for the contestation of educational goals and purposes, in which stakeholders attempt to redraw the borders of institutional control. As living institutions, schools grow and evolve in a continuous dialectic. There is an ongoing tension between what is planned, designed, created, and strategized; and the play of "unintended consequences, heterogeneous networks, ill-fitting financial and technological strategies and disorganized response" (Grosvenor, Lawn, and Rousmaniere 2000). Such cultural becoming, even of the most tightly planned interventions, is always fluid, contested, disrupted, subverted, and appropriated—in short, diverted—to a greater or lesser extent.

Even so, however, over time, certain routines, values, meanings, ways of doing and being, and so on "shake down" out of the fluid dynamics and the cultural dialectic of institutional life. Certain sediments, like standardized assessments and the strict regulation of time, consolidate, solidify, and grow. Others, like gender and racial segregation, gradually erode. Fragments bond and endure, abiding amidst the ongoing contingent resistances, contestations, and unintended outcomes of everyday practices within real (material) school sites. These collectively comprise what Hodas (1993) calls "the look-and-feel of schools" (p. 1). They are what underpin the truth in claims that time travelers from the nineteenth century could step into a classroom at the dawn of the twenty-first century and know exactly where they were, in ways they could not in a range of business, financial, productive, or administrative settings.

The values and practices that have become sedimented within school space include the pivotal role of the teacher as authoritative information source and disciplinary agent, an enduring order of hierarchy, expertise, surveillance, and accountability, regimes of assessment and ranking, subject-centered instruction, routines and architecture of physical confinement and order, age-specificity of learners, timetabled routines and procedures, and so on.

Hodas provides an interesting perspective on what is enduring and "sedimented" so far as school space is concerned and, to that extent, what is privileged over more local and immediate contingencies of preference and aspiration. He claims that in their normative capacity, schools perpetuate "the core values of the bourgeois humanism that has been developing in the West since the Enlightenment" (1993, p. xx). These include the institutional and organizational values on which the school itself is founded, which are resistant to being negotiated, compromised, or displaced by others that people—no matter how influential or visible—might happen to prefer at a given time or in a given place

School as More than Just a (Social) Technology

Schools are considerably more than social technologies alone. There are important aspects of the ways schools operate that cannot be described and explained in terms of a deliberately designed institution responding rationally to a set of established values and purposes.

As we have already mentioned, schools are dynamic sites: spaces in which contradictory purposes, organizational tensions, conflicting wills, opposing agendas, and more-or-less spontaneous and unintended events and processes play out. In addition, however, Hodas identifies two further dimensions of the identities and purposes of schools that influence what happens when innovations are introduced into, or imposed upon, school routines and practices.

The first is that schools are organizations and, as such, are interested in self-preservation. This means preserving—and defending—the way they operate. Often, defending an established modus operandi takes precedence over what might appear to outsiders as improved, more efficient or more rational ways of achieving a purpose or responding to new social conditions. Where school personnel perceive proposed improvements as disruptions or as contrary to the ethos of education as they understand it, the response will be "to relieve the stress on the organization" caused by pressure operating outside of or overwhelming the capacity of normal'channels (Hodas 1993, p. 2). As a culture, schools are not "infinitely malleable" or open to change (ibid.). To the extent that innovations, impositions, new values, and the like threaten to disrupt the established ways of the school, its personnel will resist, assimilate, subvert, or find ways of appropriating on school terms what is being proposed or imposed.

Second, as workplaces, schools are rigidly hierarchical. They have established "lines of flow of power, information, and authority"—as do all organizations (ibid.). The interests of personnel at different levels of the school's organizational culture are often in tension, if not actually opposed. Following Michael Fullan and Suzanne Stiegelbauer (1991), Hodas distinguishes three levels of power, status, and autonomy within the school organizational hierarchy. At the top are what he calls "district level administrators." Building level administrators (like principals, deputies, and, perhaps, heads of departments) are in the middle. Rank and file teachers are at the bottom. Some variations around the details may be apparent from one country to the next, but the broad contours hold.

This hierarchical order and divergence between interests across the different levels have important implications for what happens to attempts to introduce innovative practices or new technological interventions into the organizational culture of a school. For example,

A technology that reinforces existing lines of power and information is likely to be adopted (a management decision) but may or may not be implemented (a classroom level decision). The divergence of interests between managers and workers, and the potential implementation fissures along these lines is a source of much of the implementation failure of widely-touted "advances." (Hodas 1993, p. 3)

Schools and Educational Change Processes

The question of what happens when a new social technology is introduced into, imposed upon, or otherwise brought into the space of an existing and established social technology can be approached as a question of change and illuminated by change theory. In this case, our topic can be usefully informed by recent developments in educational change theory.

There are other positions on new ICTs in schools that contrast markedly with the general kind of picture painted for education systems as a whole by people like Hodas. Within the context of discussing patterns of educational change during the 1960s and 1970s, Richard Bucher and Anselm Strauss's (1976) work on how professions change throws a different light on new technologies in classrooms. Bucher and Strauss had argued that new change formulations, ideas, and inventions normally exist in several places over a period of time, but that only a few of them are adopted. As an example of the process whereby change proceeds from an initial stage of "invention" or "formulation" to a subsequent stage of "promotion" or "change implementation," it is possible to consider the case of science and math teachers responding positively to computer technology at a very early point in the development of computing (see also Goodson 2001). According to Joseph Ben-David and Randall Collins (1966), curriculum change in the form of new subjects occurs "where and when persons [become] interested in the new idea, not only as intellectual content, but also as a means of establishing a new intellectual identity and particularly a new occupational role" (p. 461). Thus, seen from this angle, science and mathematics teachers have been proactive in adopting computing into new conceptions of their subject areas because they have perceived significant possibilities for basic improvements in their occupational role and status. In other words, they envisaged change in this direction as being compatible with personal ideals, identity aspirations, and notions of a worthwhile educational project in their subject area. They recognized an important new symbolic space opening up and moved to occupy and colonize that space in ways that would enhance their existing position.

The widespread phenomenon of "technology refusal" identified by Hodas (and others, e.g., Goodson and Mangan 1995b) often contrasts markedly with this more specific case of high school science and math teachers. As Hodas notes, a good deal of the push behind introducing new technologies into classroom teaching and learning is an unveiled criticism of teachers and teacher performance: A machine can do it better (Perelman 1992; for a critical response see Robertson 1998). At the very least, efforts to technologize education are based on assumptions that computers will augment teacher knowledge and help lift learning outcomes. To the extent that this motivation highlights teacher limitations, it implies that pedagogical relations can be enhanced with the assistance of machine mediations. The rush to technologize learning often conflicts deeply with teacher identities and their personal educational concepts, ideals, and projects.

Straightforward considerations of teacher identities and roles in relation to new technologies can be enhanced further by considering recent changes in the context of educational change. Goodson (2001) distinguishes three different periods of educational change since the 1960s, and identifies general social and historical conditions under which change is more likely to gain direction and force. Goodson notes that change processes involve a number of different "segments" that may organize themselves like a coalition around a common focus, and may take on a name as a "social movement." Such names as "computers in classrooms" or "back to basics" are familiar examples. The more the segments are in harmony the more likely it is that the "social movement" will achieve force and momentum, and change will occur effectively. Three segments in particular, which Goodson calls the "internal," the "external," and the "personal," are especially important for understanding educational change.

> Internal change agents work within school settings to initiate and promote change within an external framework of support and sponsorship; external change is mandated in a top-down manner, as with the introduction of national curriculum guidelines or new state testing regimes; personal change refers to the personal beliefs and missions that individuals bring to the change process. (p. 45)

The kind of relationship that exists between segments of change processes varies from time to time and place to place. During different change periods different segments may have primacy. At some times they will be more tightly integrated and interlinked than at others. They are always related more or less closely to each other, however, since they are fundamental components of change forces and processes. From this base, it is possible to argue that during the 1960s and 1970s the internal element was largely the driving force in educational change. External "players" (like government, unions, private sector interests, and the like) largely left it to educational professionals to formulate and direct change and provided legitimating support for the directions taken.

The situation shifted from the late 1970s onwards to a period in which external change agents assumed primacy, and internal elements faced (and

continue to face) a "crisis of positionality." Their traditional "spaces" in decision-making processes had been usurped. Currently, we may be entering
a period when "the personal" (personal agency) assumes greater significance in educational change. This is a time in which "personal life politics"
are becoming increasingly powerful (Giddens 1993). In short, externally
imposed and directed change that fails to take sufficiently into account the
"missions" of internal change agents and the increasing force of personal
identity projects is likely to founder.

> A new phase of change now beckons, which acknowledges the force of per-
> sonal identity projects under post-modernity and which seeks new integra-
> tion with internal missions. Unless this new balance is achieved, change
> forces will be neither humanized nor galvanized. "Change" will stand as a
> form of political symbolic action without personal or internal commitment
> or ownership. (Goodson 2001, p. 59)

Regardless of whether such a new change phase emerges, we may be
able to benefit from examining what happens when a new social technology is projected into the space of the established social technology of
school. The fate of this new force can be explored in terms of the balance
and priority among the segments of change, and the jostling and readjust-
ments needed in accommodating this new "imposition." For if it is true
that science and math teachers embraced computing within internally led
change processes during the 1970s, it is equally true that the subsequent
policy push for computer-mediated teaching and learning emerged during that same period. At the time, external change agents were dominant
to the point of arrogance (see Mangan 1994). They worked systematically
to displace and marginalize internal change agents and were yet to discover
the forces of personal identity politics. New technologies were imposed on
schools by policy directives and in situations where teachers were notori-
ously under-prepared and under-informed with respect to using these new
digital technologies. This is still the situation in many schools.

Hence, in addition to the question of whether educators are prepared
to try and implement "computers in learning" policies, there remains the
further question of how well or efficiently they are able to integrate new
technologies into learning. What happens under these conditions may have
a lot to do with the mindsets of those involved.

The Impact of Mindsets

Mindsets are usually defined unproblematically as lenses through which we
view the world (Funk-Unrau 1999). They are "default orientations"—the
mode we automatically proceed from in approaching aspects of the world

or of everyday life. In the concept of a "mindset," however, the "set" component is interesting because it has at least three different meanings simultaneously.

First, mindsets are usually made up of *sets* of components: for example, sets of assumptions, beliefs or expectations that more or less cohere ("go together") as a set. While mindsets can usually be boiled down to a single general idea or "mode," they nonetheless accommodate multiple—and often myriad—elements within their set. Second, "mindset" trades on the idea of "set" as in "ready, set, go." They get us "set" (or set up) to respond to something in the world. Third, mindsets are "set" in the way that gelatin and concrete set. They tend to become consolidated, in the sense of being set in one's ways or views. This setting need not be permanent, although it often is or, at least, can prove to be fairly recalcitrant. Margaret Cooper and Dianne Temby (2000) emphasize this latter aspect of mindsets. They argue that when people "fail to challenge the assumptions of their worldviews from time to time and instead slip into comfortable complacency . . . they get into a thinking rut and strongly resist challenges to their views. When this happens a 'mindset' is said to exist" (p. 1).

The term "mindsets" often carries pejorative connotations of the kind implied by Cooper and Temby. From that standpoint the challenge is seen as one of trying to get people out of their mindsets and to free up their default mode of response. By the same token, though, mindsets—in the sense of lenses through which to view the world—are unavoidable. We simply could not function without them. Donna Meadows (1999) contrasts two mindsets about sustainable agriculture.

> "I guess you must be in favor of pesticides," concluded a Monsanto public relations guy, after I objected to his company's genetically engineered potato. . . . The idea that if I oppose genetic engineering, I must favor pesticides, arises from an assumption that those are the only two choices. If they were, I would probably agree that it's better to fool with genomes than to spray poisons over the countryside. But I see other choices. Plant many kinds of crops and rotate them, instead of one or two crops year after year, which make a perfect breeding ground for pests. Build up ecosystems above ground and in the soil so natural enemies rise and fall with the pests, searching and destroying with a specificity and safety and elegance that neither chemicals nor engineering can match.

Meadows recognizes her own perspective as a mindset: one that admits more than two choices. To her it is every bit as much a mindset as that of the Monsato PR guy. When approached from this standpoint, the aim is to seek optimally effective and adaptable mindsets rather than to try and avoid having them at all. The art is to know when to evolve; when to move on. With respect to the emergence of a world in which new ICTs are pervasive, Richard Lanham (1994) provides an interesting line of argument that goes to the heart of the issue of mindsets as it will concern us in this book.

Lanham is one of a growing number of theorists and researchers who see "attention" as the scarce or precious resource in the emerging economy of the information society. This new economy is becoming known as "the attention economy" (Adler 1997; Goldhaber 1997; Lanham 1994). Besides being scarce, the key point about attention so far as Lanham is concerned is that it is nonmaterial. He claims that when the most precious resource in an economy is nonmaterial "the economic doctrines, social structures, and political systems that evolved in a world devoted to the service of matter become rapidly ill-suited to cope with the new situation" (Wriston 1997, cited in Lanham 1994, p. 1). In a manner similar to Goldhaber (1997), John Perry Barlow (2000), and Nicholas Negroponte (1995), among others, Lanham insists we cannot continue to apply concepts, laws, practices, and the like that were developed to deal with the economic world of goods to the emerging economic world of information. This is basically an argument that a mindset appropriate to a world concerned primarily with the physical or material (what Negroponte calls a world of "atoms") is ill-adapted to orienting us in a world in which what is increasingly important is non-material (what Negroponte calls a world of "bits").

Lanham sees various casualties of this phenomenon. For example, some of the most cherished investments of researchers and teachers in the areas of literacy and communication are seriously undermined within information space. A theory of communication based on stuff presupposes a model of simple exchange, whereby a package of thought and feeling is transferred from one body and place to another or others. The same communication model, says Lanham (1994), employs a "Clarity-Brevity-Sincerity" style of prose and expression. He argues that this model no longer applies. The transaction within an attention economy is no longer "simply the rational market . . . beloved by the economists of stuff." Rather, people bring with them to the free market of ideas "a complex calculus of pleasure" and "make all kinds of purchases" in the attention economy.

In spatial terms, the information model is revolutionizing practices of literacy and thinking, which Lanham illustrates by reference to the library. No longer can librarians see their role as one of "facilitating thinking done elsewhere," as was the case in the age of lending out books. Lanham distinguishes his own mindset and position here from that of a librarian with whom he had corresponded. The librarian maintained that in the age of information the role of librarians remains essentially unchanged. It is still a matter of "maintaining the signifiers, and leaving the decryption of the signifieds to the readers" (p. 1).

In opposition to this, Lanham argues that in a world of superabundant information, thinking involves generating what he calls "attention structures." These are frames and organizers that facilitate paying attention to data so that we can turn it into something useful. The contemporary problem is that in the electronic age of "the rich signal" (digital code that can come at us as multiple media at vast volumes) we are so bombarded with data that it can be difficult to know what to attend to in order to use the data productively. Users of data need attention structures that they cannot necessarily produce themselves. From his different mindset, Lanham believes that libraries and librarians are in the thick of this situation. He argues that the role of the librarian must change to include the role of generating attention structures for the information they deal in and with. They need to become involved in building "thinking facilitation" into the data they purvey.

Whatever our personal views on the kinds of positions argued by people like Lanham, there is now widespread recognition of the escalating centrality of the virtual within the everyday lives of millions of people within societies like our own. The increasing importance of virtual realities is generating a crisis for mindsets grounded in the physical-industrial-material order of modernity. In some of their recent work, Colin Lankshear and Chris Bigum (2000) draw on the work of John Perry Barlow (e.g., Barlow 2000; see also Tunbridge 1995; and chapter 5 in this book) to substantiate a distinction between two broad types of mindsets pertaining to education and new technologies. Behind this distinction is the idea that space has been fractured in the current period.

The notion of the fracturing of space involves the dramatic emergence and explosion of cyberspace as a distinctively new space co-existing with physical space and, particularly, with physical space constructed in industrial terms. The divergence in mindsets is between those who continue to see the world in terms—or through perspectives—forged within the context of industrial mastery and constitution of the physical world, and those who see the world as inherently different from before, on account of the impact of the industrial technology revolution and a new informational or cyberspatial paradigm emerging with it (Lankshear and Bigum 2000). More specifically, the divergence is between people who see the world as being more or less the same as before, only more "technologized," and those who see the world as now being fundamentally changed, in large part because of the way new technologies have impacted it.

Consequently, one way in which we can try to describe and understand what happens when a new technology intrudes upon the space of an existing social technology is by focusing on the play of mindsets within concrete situations. For example, it is very common to find an "old wine in new bottles" syndrome when researching attempts to integrate new technologies into classroom learning, as will be discussed in chapter 4. Nonetheless, it is becoming easier to find examples where people willfully bring new mindsets to their social practices involving new technologies.

Several ICT theorists have produced "level" theories that classify technology applications as being low, medium, or high in their level of interactivity, or in their innovative use of new possibilities (e.g., Maddux, Johnson, and Willis 2001; Schwier and Misanchuk 1993). Not surprisingly, examples at the high end of the scale are not common in the field of education.

In his account of the creation and rise of Amazon.com, Robert Spector (2000) recounts the perspective taken by Amazon.com's founder, Jeff Bezos. At the time when Bezos was wanting to establish the kind of enterprise that would eventually materialize into Amazon.com, he expressed his interest in the possibility of "hook[ing] up with a technology company," where he could chase his real passion—"second-phase" automation.

Bezos has described second-phase automation as "the common theme that has run through my life. The first phase of automation is where you use technology to do the same old business processes, but just faster and more efficiently." A typical first phase of automation in the e-commerce field would be barcode scanners and point-of-sale systems. With the internet "you're doing the same process you've always done, but just more efficiently." He described the second phase of automation as "when you can fundamentally change the underlying business process and do things in a completely new way. So it's more of a revolution instead of an evolution." (Spector 2000, p. 16)

Bezos's notion of second-phase automation implies conscious mobilization of meta-level understandings of new technologies and new times, and the will to "enact" new kinds of projects and create new social practices using online environments. Customers go to Amazon.com's website and browse books by category, or by searching for particular topics, titles, or authors. Each web page for each book has space for readers to post reviews of the book, and an evaluation rating scale for readers to post their ratings of the book. Amazon also recommends books you might like, based on your previous purchases or on information you have provided. It even offers cash prizes to customers who write the first reviews for listed books, music CDs, DVDs, toys, electronic gadgets, and so on.

The company has greatly diversified its range of activities during the past two years. It now provides an auction service and has developed a range of "sister" sites that sell, among other things, health and beauty products, electronics, software, household items, music, and toys. Its website incorporates a range of strategies to encourage customers to buy as much as possible. Its stated mission is "to use the internet to transform book buying into the fastest, easiest, and most enjoyable shopping experience possible" (Amazon.com, cited in Spector 2000, p. 1). This reflects a very different mindset from seeing the world as being the same, only more technologized. It approaches new communications and information technologies from the standpoint that these new technologies are integral to the scale and direction of contemporary change.

Playmakers

Manuel Castells (2000) explains that new information technologies are not simply tools but are also, and crucially, processes to be developed. This has to do with the nature and role of knowledge and information within the current revolution. According to Castells, the information technology revolution and the emergence of a knowledge society are not principally constituted by the centrality of knowledge and information. New forms of knowledge and information are important in all such moments of major productive and developmental change. Rather, at the heart of the current revolution is the way knowledge and information are applied to knowledge generation and information processing/communication devices. Castells refers here to a "cumulative feedback loop between innovation and the uses of innovation." He notes that, since the 1970s,

> the uses of telecommunications technologies have gone through three distinct stages: automation of tasks, experimentation of uses, reconfiguration of applications. In the first two stages technological innovation progressed through learning *by using*. . . . In the third stage, the users learned technology *by doing* and ended up reconfiguring the networks, and finding new applications. (p. 32, emphasis in original)

Everyday diffusion of the new technology amplifies its powers as it is appropriated and redefined by users through doing—which is what Castells means by identifying the new information technologies as processes to be developed as well as tools to be used. Successful new applications add economic and technological value, bestowing advantage and elite status on their inventors. This is because of the close relationship that now exists between creating and manipulating symbols (cultural activity) and the ability to produce goods and services (productive or economic activity). Within the contemporary context, then, elites learn by *doing,* not by *using*—where "elites" are construed as those who generate high additions to value. By the same token, users can become doers "by taking control of technology, as in the case of the internet" (ibid.).

This seems to be the way of the world from the standpoint of contemporary playmakers in areas outside education. They operate as far as possible outside spaces of "sedimented ways," often viewing established cultural traditions and values like so much clutter on a hard disk: to be expunged or, at the very least, "defragged." It is different for people working in schools. Precisely how different it is constitutes the focus of what we explore from diverse angles in the chapters that follow. In those chapters, we will pursue many of the themes introduced here: the struggle to define and claim new educational spaces; the collision of established cultures of schooling with new cultures of computing; the impact of mindsets and personal politics as these struggles play themselves out. By looking at specific instances of the encounter between school culture and technoculture, we will be able to see familiar patterns of imposition and resistance, but also movement toward genuinely new forms of teaching and learning.

2

CULTURE CLASH IN
COMPUTERIZED CLASSROOMS

IN THIS CHAPTER, WE FOCUS ON THE INTRODUCTION of computers into high school classrooms in Ontario, Canada. Many studies of computer introduction focus on issues of technical implementation: issues of how people learn the techniques and, indeed, the "language" of computers. This concentration reflects a certain definition of the problems surrounding the introduction of ICTs into schools. Essentially, the problems are seen as those of overcoming the considerable challenges presented by selection of the hardware and software, technology installation and maintenance, and staff training and development. The methodology of such research, whether qualitative or quantitative, reflects this definition of the problem in its focus. And, as with all research, the definition of the problem and the methodological focus have a great deal of influence on what we "find."

In the research to be discussed here, beginning in Ontario in the early 1990s and spanning a decade, we sought to broaden our conception of the problem and our methodological focus (our "lens of inquiry"—see Goodson and Mangan 1995a; 1996b). Our approach reflected a move from an emphasis on the issues pertaining to technical implementation to a wider purview of the "computerization" of schooling. Thus, what we report here will reflect our interest in the introduction of computers as not so much a technical issue, but rather as a cultural issue. Because we value the "cultural" in any research investigation, our express goal has been to develop research methodologies that embrace not only the technical, but also the cultural dimensions of new technologies.

In our Ontario-based study, for example, we focused on the ways in which subject-area teachers—whether of geography, art, or technology—responded to the introduction of computers into schools (and to the tacit expectation that these teachers would make good use of these computers). We found that by not just studying the technical issues associated with managing computers within schools, but by also explicitly focusing on the cultural dimension of this event, we were able to identify a number of ways in which the sudden introduction of new technologies into a school invoked "culture clashes" that significantly interrupted or altered the character of the adoption of new technologies into teachers' everyday classroom practices.

First, we judged that the introduction of computers by the provincial government was a form of symbolic action; a drive related to issues of school governance and control (Goodson and Mangan 1992; 1996a). Here we found concerns and questions voiced by teachers regarding who governs schooling and curriculum: Should it be political and bureaucratic state cultures, or professional cultures comprised of teachers and administrators?

Second, and over and above this issue, was the related problem for teachers of having to create and be part of a new "performative" or "audit culture." New "performative" societies, of course, are linked inextricably to the (new) technological preparation of a work force. Performativity is always a case of demonstrating that certain benchmarks, quotas, and goals have been achieved, without due attention to the quality of products or the process attending each "performance" (see Lyotard 1984). The concept of performativity also helps us to identify and anticipate a new division of labor in the "new work order" (an appropriate analogy here would be the introduction of new machines being allied to the establishment of the factory system of production and production management—see Gee, Hull, and Lankshear 1996). By bringing in a technological vision of society and underpinning this with testing and accountability regimes, a "performative culture" is put in place—part of a general cultural plan of ensuring that students grow up corporate and ready to fit seamlessly into a (technological) vision of consumption and continuous economic growth. This can at times clash with teachers' goals for and assumptions about the role of schooling in students' lives.

Third, another potential axis of "culture clash" for teachers lies at the intersection of traditional school subjects and this new work order. The school subject is a carefully defined curriculum space. In some ways, traditional school subjects were designed at the time and in the form of the old economy of industrial work. Subjects were enclosures of the word, based on subject disciplines that were like an industrial technology for getting things done (Lankshear, Peters, and Knobel 1996). Most school subjects traditionally reflected widely accepted "disciplines" of knowledge (e.g., science, literature, philosophy) and underwrote the idea of the teacher as subject expert, reciter of facts, a figure to be listened to and directed by

(Goodson 1992a; Hirst 1983). Replacing the subject teacher in these roles with a computer program represents a substantial cultural shift. In one sense, it is related to the shift from bounded, work-disciplined industrial space to post-industrial, dispersed, increasingly nonmaterial space and logic. The subject teacher still lives in a material world, but the new cultural logic is encapsulated in the computer.

Fourth, and related directly to the previous point, we have also encountered a culture clash between antecedent subject cultures and computerized cultures of schooling. In the following account, we watch an established teacher of geography confronting "computer culture," and how other teachers represent this particular clash of cultures. As a subplot, we see how our research methods both succeed and fail in embracing the complexity required to identify, map, and explain culture clashes within the context of computerized schooling.

Constructing a Research Methodology

Trying to assess the culture of educational computing brings us back to what and how we "watch" the process of ICT introduction. In a series of research projects led by Ivor Goodson, first in Ontario (funded by the Ontario Ministry of Education, 1989–1992) and later in Ontario and New York State (funded by the Spencer Foundation, 1998–2003), the researchers paid close attention to both the ethics and epistemology of the fieldwork (see Goodson and Mangan 1996b). The project teams were committed to extending their research focus beyond considerations of technical competence and implementation alone. To this end, we decided to focus on "the person"—in this case, the teacher or student—as being the center of the action, rather than the software programs they use, or the configuration of machines available to them, and so on. In this way we could examine closely the ways in which culture clashes are mediated, negotiated, and monitored by people as they go about their everyday educational life and work.

In short, we decided to construct our methodology from within the tradition of life history study; an approach first perfected and widely practiced in the Chicago sociology department of the 1930s (see Goodson 1992b). We began with classroom observations and ethnographic fieldwork and, alongside this, conducted a range of life history interviews over the three years of each project. At the time, this marked a radical break from conventional studies of new technology use in schools.

In what follows, we will begin by discussing what we found in terms of the relationship between teachers' personal and professional lives, and between their teaching styles and the "imposition" of new technologies, in order to highlight the complexities involved in computerizing schools. We will show how subject subcultures are instantiated and reproduced through teachers' organizational and pedagogical practices, and how this can set up a potential clash with the culture of computing.

Then, in the remainder of the chapter, we will focus primarily on one subject teacher from the first project: "Jim," a geography specialist (all names used here are pseudonyms). A retroactive examination of his reactions over the two years of the project, set within the context of our broad focus on professional cultures, and viewed within a wider sense of a person's life, allowed us to reformulate our initial "representations" of a teacher's response to computers. We began to see the general culture clash between school subject cultures and computer culture, but also the kinds of life-history influences that cannot be ignored in the study of any educational innovation. In the last section of this chapter, we will return again to Jim to show how complex the analysis of culture clash can be.

Teaching Styles and Teachers' Lives

In most cases, teachers perceive their pedagogical style as a limited arena of personal choice in which they have the freedom and power to make only minor variations in state-mandated curriculum and school-shaped pedagogy. These variations are constrained by both the fundamental culture of teaching and the subject subculture (Goodson 1995; 2001).

Nevertheless, we did find interesting juxtapositions of personal style and cultural factors emerging from our data. For example, with regard to the use of educational technology and media, one of the participating geography teachers preferred to use 16-mm films in his teaching, while the others relied more on models, maps, and blackboards. The history teachers all made extensive use of videos. Diane, one of the family studies teachers, regularly used overheads and filmstrips, but few other technological media.

As another example, the participating teachers varied the format of discussions and Socratic questioning within their respective classrooms, with some relying on volunteer respondents or electing respondents themselves, some encouraging student-led discussions, and others making significant use of teacher-led quizzes. There were also observed differences in the degree of "assigned co-operation" in each classroom: some participating teachers encouraged more group work and student interaction than others. Similarly, some teachers seemed more inclined to rely on peer coaching and tutoring than others did. Some had formal peer-evaluation procedures; others had none.

More than one teacher said that teaching style was an expression of a teacher's personality. If this is true, the implication is that a change in style would require nothing less than a change in personality as well, not to mention a change in culture (see Rossman, Corbett, and Firestone 1988). The difficulty with enforcing such changes was sometimes acknowledged by the teachers themselves, as in this explanation by social studies teacher, Elliot:

> I think that if I categorize my teaching style, it's been fairly obviously teacher-directed. . . . But I think if I want to use the computers more, with three in the room, I've got to be more flexible in letting kids work at a different pace, work on different things at different times. . . . So it means sitting down and doing some fairly drastic revisions of ways I've done things in the past, to tailor it more to individuals or to small groups.

In the life-history interviews we conducted, we found that participating teachers often expressed two basic philosophies: first, that they cared deeply about their students and were interested in opening up some form of novel learning experiences for them; and second, that their teaching styles derived directly from their concept of education and its intersection with their personal lifestyles. Diane, for instance, said that she likes "everything up front" and tries to teach the same way. Harry, a social studies teacher, described himself as "content oriented" and said he structured his classes accordingly.

Some of the more senior teachers, particularly from social studies, indicated that they relied more on experience than on preparation to get them through their classes. For instance, Elliott once said: "I find it fairly easy to come in some days unprepared, then fall back on my experience, or fall back on the fact that I know a certain page in the textbook has some information that's necessary, and to have the kids read it." For us, this was an explicit indication of these teachers' complete immersion in, and identification with, their subject subculture. For them, teaching their subject seemed to come naturally and hardly required conscious preparation.

The implications of this close identification of teachers' lives with their professional practice, and the impact of the introduction of computers upon that practice, is a complex topic that we explored in a number of ways. In research reported elsewhere (see Goodson and Mangan 1991; 1995b; Goodson, Mangan, and Rhea 1991), we found that computer use seemed to impose a more uniform teaching style. In a quantitative analysis of classroom observation data, we discovered a statistically significant impact on such areas as the proportion of time devoted to small-group activities, and in student participation, when computerized classrooms were compared with more traditional settings (see the Appendix for a summary of the statistical results).

We began to see that the forms of interaction favored by the introduction of computers into secondary schools cut across the established pedagogical patterns of existing subject subcultures. This finding confirmed our suspicions of the potential for a culture clash. Given the extent to which teachers identified with the teaching styles traditionally associated with their subject subcultures, we noted they might be reluctant to adopt a technology that seems incompatible with those subcultures. To understand exactly what forms this culture clash might take, we returned to a re-examination of our interview data, especially among those teachers who seemed to articulate clearly the meaning of their subject subculture, and among those less than enthusiastic about the introduction of new technologies.

Teaching Subjects and the Introduction of Computers

In Ontario as elsewhere, the evolution of high-school subject subcultures preceded the introduction of the computer by over a century. As both bodies of knowledge and institutionalized professional groups, subject subcultures represent the terrain into which a new (alien) force, the computer, is being introduced. In the interviews and group discussions we conducted, teachers articulated the characteristics of these subcultures in a number of ways.

Although they may not have used the term themselves, teachers talked about their subject subcultures in many ways. For instance, with regard to patterns of classroom organization and control, Wendy, an art teacher, noted that "People don't face the front in art rooms . . . they're facing each other in a circle around the room . . . and they get up and they move around all the time." Although she felt that art requires freedom of movement and expression, Wendy was also concerned with classroom control, the sine qua non of public school teaching. She noted that her classroom environment was "terribly unstable I'd say . . . most of my job is people control. It'd be nice if it was teaching art, just teaching art, but it isn't." For Wendy, the insertion of computers into such an environment had the potential to either exacerbate or relieve problems of control. She viewed independent in-class computer use as one way of keeping students "very busy, very happy, very absorbed in something productive. . . . That's always a big plus."

Likewise, within family studies, the antecedent subject subculture favored a classroom where different students were occupied with different tasks. Because an individualized classroom environment already existed, the introduction of computers seemed reasonably unproblematic:

Betty: Well, in family studies we often have different groups doing different things.

Interviewer: So that won't be a major adaptation for you, you'll be able to just . . .

Betty: No. Especially the sewing project. I mean their rate of doing things is so varied in that some finish before the others have cut it out! So you have all these people at different stages, so I think it will be handy for that. You can enrich the program for the faster ones . . . in a way that, you know, I think they would find interesting, rather than just another sewing assignment.

In other subjects, however, the pattern of "whole class" teaching posed great problems for those wishing to introduce computers. We found this particularly the case in some history and geography classrooms. Harry, when asked how computers fit into his social studies classroom, replied:

Harry: It's an extra right now, yes.

Interviewer: It's not in the fabric in your class planning really?

Harry: And I'm finding more and more it's difficult to actually think of ways to include it for an entire class. And I think one of the limitations is that there are only three of them in the room. I can't count on having the three here or the three in the geography room at any given time. And it's also a reflection that I haven't really sat down and tried to organize a class computer-related program.

Although the antecedent subject subculture provides an important variable in the adoption of computers in the classroom, there are commonalties as well as differences in the ways teachers introduce computers into their lessons. On the whole, we found very few examples of teachers fundamentally reworking their lesson plans and pedagogy. In addition to the common attitude expressed by Harry—that he had to fit the computer into his existing routine—teachers also spoke in terms of the computer as "just another tool," as "just another way of learning" (see also Carlson 1991; Moll 2001). What these phrases summarized for us was the belief that computers would not substantially change the way participating teachers conducted their lessons and approached classroom learning. Commercial art teacher, Barb, stated that:

I would like seven to ten computers in here, because I know a lot of times we don't always have to be on the computer and, in the business, *the computer is just another tool. It's just another medium.* And if you go to a studio . . . now what they do, you know, they go to the drafting table, work something up, work up the graphics, go to the computer, do what has to be done by the computer. . . . They bring it back if they have to paste something up or, you know, if they have to put in an illustration or whatever, they have to scan something, they scan it . . . so, *basically it's just another tool.* (emphasis added)

Thus, participating teachers generally conceived of the computer as being used to modify parts of their routine existing practices. Small bits of existing lesson plans are replaced by computerized bits, but the basic objectives and structure remain much the same. Carl, a drafting teacher, described his approach this way:

Let's suppose that we have this *CAD-Tutor* in place. . . . It would be a very good thing when I've mastered it and I can sit down with three students and say, "I want you to do this exercise and this is how you basically go through doing it." Give them the demonstration, and then have them do it. And then rotate another three kids through. . . . Now I will eliminate something from the curriculum in order to insert that little piece, okay? So that gives me the time. So I'll kill something off that I don't think is as necessary as the *CAD-Tutor.* And the same will apply to the electronics program. . . . Something that I think is more usefully done on the computer, I will eliminate the old method to make the space.

The computers were most enthusiastically taken up where they fit in with existing practice and caused no substantial changes in content or pedagogy. In art, for instance:

Interviewer: So, do you feel that you've made any major or drastic changes to your lesson plans, or your teaching style, to accommodate these computers?
Wendy: I don't think so. I think it fits in quite nicely in the classroom.
Interviewer: Uh-huh.
Wendy: I don't think I've had to do too many things differently because of it. . . .
Interviewer: So you feel they fit in all right in that way, as well?
Wendy: Oh, they especially fit in because of that set-up in the classroom. It's not mostly a teacher talking for half an hour, and students then doing their work. It's everybody working, and me helping them solve problems. And the computer is . . . just presents a new series of problems to be solved by the students too. . . .

This teacher, then, felt that the computers, as delivered, did not disrupt the culture of her classroom. By contrast, teachers in other subjects sometimes felt they had to modify their use of computers to ensure that they did not disrupt the established subculture. Harry summarized this pattern of the co-option of computers into the existing framework:

Interviewer: If we get geography software, is that going to solve the problem of your teaching style and your classroom management, or are there going to be new problems down the road, even if there is geography software?

Harry: We're always going to have to adapt whatever they give us to our own teaching style, or our own content orientation, or whatever the case is. Because I dare say there will never be a program that fits me exactly, or what I want to accomplish. It may come close, but I don't think there will ever be one that I can say: "Hey, that's perfect for me, and let's go with it." I may be wrong there, but what I've seen, I don't think so.

Overall, then, what seems to be at stake here are the traditional patterns of subject knowledge and subject learning. Subjects are well-established and reasonably well-delineated bodies of knowledge and social practices. They carry with them assumptions about "worthwhile knowledge," "good students," "effective teaching," and "excellent results." Potentially, the computer can enhance these established social procedures or disrupt them. Teachers can co-opt the technology, they can adapt it or adapt to it, but, in some instances, they can also "surrender" to it. In extreme cases, this can lead to the actual replacement of subject learning by technical learning— a replacement, in short, of the academic by the vocational. Not all teachers resist this state of affairs. Ed, an enthusiastic innovator with computers, described the transition:

Yes, it has changed the way I teach geography. I've downplayed content and moved to teaching skills—in a way, I see myself teaching computing first and geography second . . . and that's fair enough I suppose, because knowing computing will get them jobs . . . whereas geography . . . well what can I say?

Of course, this view expresses an extreme pendulum swing, directly away from subject teaching to technical training. In the process, Ed was actually led to denigrate the relevance of his own subject specialty. But the quote also neatly captures the "either/or" view that is prevalent among many teachers. Either I can co-opt the computer to fit broadly what I am already doing (and think I do well), or my existing subject and practice is overthrown and I become a technical trainer. Most of the teachers in our project were still ambivalent about this transition, but very few teachers articulated the view common in the rhetoric of guidelines and computer publicity: that computers will revolutionize classrooms and massively enhance the efficiency and scope of subject teaching and learning (see Levinson 1990).

The co-optation of computers by subject teachers is an example of a very common response to innovations and to the lack of sensitivity toward teachers that often accompanies them. As one teacher pointed out: "if you look at the history of computer use in secondary schools, it's like everything else, it's been brought on us from above." Initiatives from above are not always seen by teachers as well-informed or, indeed, well-intentioned. They are sometimes viewed as essentially political responses to powerful pressure groups in society (Cole 1990). There were certainly teachers who saw it as politically expedient to introduce computers to accommodate business and economic interests (Robertson 1998). Such an interpretation could be applied to the quote above, in which a teacher sees his customary practice being displaced by vocational demands.

Teachers often respond pragmatically to innovations from above. In general, they co-opt the initiatives and continue broadly as before (see Fullan, Miles and Anderson 1988). In an earlier study (see Goodson 1980, p. 257), one teacher summarized the general response to new guidelines in this way: "The teacher searches out how to go on doing what has always been done in the new context." The question in another teacher's words was: "How can I do what I've always been doing in a new context?" This teacher spoke of responding to the new guidelines in terms of "reshuffling his pack of cards" (ibid.).

With the introduction of computers, we found evidence of reshuffling the pack of cards, but little evidence of anybody trying a new game. It is possible for the culture of computing to colonize some areas of the curriculum. In most areas, however, the antecedent subject subculture in effect colonizes the computer, and uses it to teach the existing subject in the existing way. In the face of established practice, the computer becomes "just another tool."

Introducing Computers:
Studying a Subject Teacher's Life and Work

Having looked at some of the general trends among the Ontario high-school classrooms we studied, we still need to ask: Does the lens of the antecedent subject subculture account for all the various forms of accommodation, resistance, co-optation, and adoption that we encountered? Although it certainly illuminated differences among teachers of different subjects, we also found a range of responses within subject subcultures, leading us to ask what other factors might be at work.

By including life-history interviews and participant reviews of our findings, we attempted to account for the widest possible range of influences. Our methodology was based on the realization that, for most in the profession, teaching is a profound expression of individual commitments, beliefs, and interpersonal styles. It was not entirely surprising, then, to discover that some of the participants who did not seem to fit well into the overall patterns emerging from our data were in fact experiencing very different life situations outside of the school environment.

Our first data on Jim, a geography teacher, were collected toward the end of the first semester of the project, and focused on his response to being invited to join the project. Recruitment of participating teachers had been left up to the school principals, and Jim indicated that he had not joined up entirely voluntarily. The interviewer asked: "So it wasn't explained to you how they happened to pick you or why they landed on you rather than someone else in the department?" Jim replied: "No, I was just stopped in the hall by the principal . . . and it sounded good at the time, but I regretted after that I had done it, okay?" He followed up this statement of reluctance with the admission that he just was not ready to take up computers: "I've had a sinking feeling that this was going to happen. I went to the first number of meetings, but it did fall off after. . . . And it's, I must admit, totally fallen off right now. So, I'm gonna have to pull myself up by the bootstraps and start again next fall."

The interesting part of this first interview is how Jim, right from the beginning, struck a note of reservation—"that sinking feeling"—which could sometimes express itself as "resistance," but might, from a whole-life perspective, be infinitely more complex. Interestingly, one of the other participating teachers commented on how she had found the initial meeting a little intimidating, with various leaders in computer implementation present. But Jim did not seem to feel that way about it at all when asked:

> No, no. I try not to let people intimidate me . . . if at all possible. I was there as a volunteer, I wasn't being paid. They wouldn't—there's no threat on my life. I mean, they're not going to cut me off or anything. So they can say, "You're doing a crappy job." That's fine . . . [or] give me a pat on the back, but it's not going to change my salary, it's not going to change my position. . . . I'm the one involved, so, you know, I don't find people intimidate me.

In some ways, our response to Jim was not unlike the way in which teachers come to stereotype and sort their students in the first few days of a school year. One of our first impressions was that he was a "resister." One of the principal researchers in this project was well known for his "Luddite" predilections, and other members of the research team commented regularly to him, "We think we've found you a resister," or "Hey, Jim's the Luddite you've been looking for!" Although these comments were made as jokes, they nonetheless expressed serious aspects of the truth: Sometimes, Jim himself seemed to express an "anti-new-technologies" position quite openly:

> Interviewer: One thing that some teachers express concern about is that using computers is an imposition of a more uniform curriculum. In other words, you can't alter the computer curriculum to the same extent that you could play around with your own lesson plans and your own teaching materials, and so forth. Do you see that as a danger in any way?
>
> Jim: No, because . . . not in my lifetime. The computer isn't going to take my place.
>
> Interviewer: No?
>
> Jim: No way!
>
> Interviewer: You don't think it will limit your freedom either though?
>
> Jim: It'll limit your freedom if you become a slave to it and enter [a place where] everything centers around the computer. Then, yes, your freedom is gone. But as far as I'm concerned, my lack of using it, is pretty indicative right now that maybe I'm not going to let somebody else—something else—interfere with me. No, I've always thought of it as a super supplement to other things that go on in the classroom, other types of lessons, okay? . . . It's not going to take my place. At least, not in seven years.

The significance of the "seven years" comment became evident later. In the exchange reported above, though, Jim's position in relation to his teaching and computers seems very clear. At other times, he seemed to present a more ambivalent, perhaps more complex view:

> Interviewer: You said that the teaching aids and AV material and things like that have changed. How do you feel computers fit into that?
>
> Jim: Well, it's the next change that I've got to swallow. As I've admitted to you before, I'm still kind of frightened of it because I haven't gotten into the swing of it yet. And it's going to start very soon and I'm crossing my fingers that I'm not going to fall on my face. If I fall on my face, I'm still going to live, so I'm not going to worry about it. But it's absolutely so useful a tool that it's got to come, and I've got to just break my back and get away from maybe old-fashioned things that I've been doing and get on with the new, because all the kids coming out of high school should have some degree of expertise in computers. And I'm not going to preach about geography being so important that it's absolutely necessary, but just the application of computers for a lot of jobs, for the simple reason that geography is not going to be something they're going to be working with for the rest of their lives.

Based on comments such as these, and our point of view at the time, we saw Jim as a resister who expressed some ambivalence every now and then. In his actions, however, we felt that Jim's "real" position was obvious: again and again in the first year, he was "just too busy" to actually introduce computers into his classroom or go to the computer laboratory with his class. He had told us he was "frightened" of "falling on his face" when using computers with his students, and his actions confirmed this. But he nonetheless regularly declared that in the summer he would buy his own computer and develop some "stuff" for his class. In the end, he did nothing during that first year, and our fieldnotes bear testament to our growing conviction that Jim was not going to "buy into" computers. In short, we began to form a clear and categorical opinion, through observation, interviews, and deductive reasoning, that Jim was a new-technology "resister."

If, for the research team, Jim was "our resister," to his colleagues, Jim was a "beached whale," "a burnt-out case," "clapped out and ready to retire" (their terms). They directly and openly expressed the belief that Jim would "never" take up computers. A fieldworker's notes recorded this conversation with the geography head at Jim's school:

[Steve] wanted to know what was going to happen to geography in the project. Jim hasn't used the lab yet and, as far as Steve is concerned, is never going to use it. [Steve] said that [Jim] will tell us that he is going to use it, but he'll come up with excuse after excuse and never use it. [Steve] knows, because he's been through it with [Jim] before, with no success. He is concerned that Jim will be representing all geographers in our reports. I assured [Steve] that that would not be so, but he felt uncomfortable with the situation. He said that he didn't want to push us into anything, but it might be a good idea to visit his classes as well. I told him what Jim told us of his plans for this year, but that he has just been too busy so far. He said that it was true, but Jim will always be too busy with other things to find time to use the computer.

In an interview, Steve said this of earlier efforts to introduce Jim to computer technology:

There were geography teachers who were already involved in dealing with computers, but not on this level. Not on a level where we can actually teach kids using the computers, because they don't have them. And this was an opportunity to actually have enough computers to really use them in the classroom. So I wanted geography involved. It didn't have to be me particularly. But I'd already tried to get Jim involved with the Commodore [computer], and I mean, I'm not talking about a one-shot try. We tried over and over, every professional-development day we had there for a while, we had at least something involving, you know, getting them hands-on a computer. And nothing happened. And I knew that that was likely to happen again.

As the research developed and interim reports emerged, both the research team and Steve ultimately agreed that Jim was representative of a type.

> Interviewer: Whatever the history behind it, I'm sort of glad that we've got Jim, because I think one of the things that happens too often in these evaluation projects is that you only get really enthusiastic, and sometimes, people with a great deal of background knowledge, as your own.
> Steve: Yes, that's right.
> Interviewer: And it creates a sort of artificial situation. I mean, one thing that I think is going to be useful to our evaluation is to try to figure out what the sort of sources of resistance or reluctance for people like Jim are. Because I don't think that you can expect everybody to embrace computer use in schools with open arms.
> Steve: Nope. He certainly proved that. No, I agree. As a research tool you have to look at the whole spectrum and he's certainly part of that spectrum. There is no question about it. But at the same time, if you were going to, you know, once you'd established that, there is an awful lot of information that came out of things, that somebody who is using the computers could provide what he'll never be able to provide you with.

So, by this stage, the researchers and Jim's colleagues had more or less come to a consensus on Jim. Although we did not want to "psychoanalyze" him, by the end of the first year our fieldnotes contained the following list of factors that seemed to combine to account for his reluctance to get involved with computers:

- Personal insecurity: habits of methodical preparation; fear of being unable to completely master or control the material during a classroom presentation; inability to completely control the material presented by the programs.
- Established teaching patterns: related to above, his presentations seem very uniform, semester to semester; he has chosen certain teaching aids that he has used for up to twenty years without change, "Socratic" style.
- Personal relationship with students: Jim likes to get to know them personally; he jokes a lot with them, makes individual eye contact in every class; acts in a quite fatherly manner toward most of them.
- Individualized treatment: Jim has repeatedly affirmed his disinterest in marking programs, because he feels there are intangible considerations

that must go into a student's final grade; he feels computers are too insensitive to the individual needs and circumstances of each student.

- Technophobia: Jim has repeatedly described himself as "old-fashioned," by which he means not only that he uses old-fashioned teaching techniques, but that he is committed to a traditional concept of literacy; he emphasizes the need to be able to write well, and to deal with maps and written material; he may be suspicious that computers undermine that traditional literate culture.

If we had relied solely on observations and recorded conversations, our interpretations of Jim would have ended there—neatly packaged and unassailable. However, by now, we had completed and were transcribing Jim's life-history interviews. Consistent with our methodology of checking our analyses back with the sources, some of the "burnt-out case" hypotheses were gently raised and discussed in these interviews.

> Interviewer: I should probably know this from earlier interviews, but it's slipped my mind: how close to retirement are you?
> Jim: Seven years.
> Interviewer: Seven years?
> Jim: Well, five to seven years.
> Interviewer: So, it's not just around the corner.
> Jim: No.
> Interviewer: Because I mean . . . if it were me, I think I might wonder about whether the investment in learning something as complex and as big as computer-assisted learning at this stage was going to pay off for me in the few remaining years of my career. Do you think that's part of it, at all?
> Jim: No.
> Interviewer: No? You are still interested in new . . . ?
> Jim: Seven years would be my ninety factor [which would allow early retirement], okay? If I was totally fed-up or ill or something with the other . . . age fifty-five, with penalty. . . . So no, in terms of a fiscal investment, I don't think so. I can't say my wife and I are poor, so it's not that.

Despite being offered the opportunity to blame his reluctance on his approaching retirement, Jim demurred. As the project wore on, however, we began finally to see new explanations for Jim's actions. In January of the third year of the project, quite suddenly, the fieldnotes changed. One researcher wrote:

> During my interview with Jim, he mentioned that it was his birthday, and that he was fifty-one as of the day of the interview. This had the effect of

retroactively explaining a lot of earlier stuff. I had just read an article by Tom Brokaw in *Esquire* about the trauma of turning fifty, and it suddenly struck me that, all during the earlier parts of the research project, Jim had been approaching, or living through, the age of fifty. His comments about feeling tired, worn out, and old-fashioned suddenly leapt into sharp focus. His generally troubled and distracted air may have something to do with this. And, not least, the fact that he survived his fiftieth year, and that that particular crisis is now behind him, may have paved the way for him to finally move ahead with a challenging new project that he had been putting off for months.

Other matters also emerged in these interviews. We learned that, in addition to turning 50, Jim's dad had died some years ago, and Jim was spending a lot of time visiting his ill mother.

> Jim: My father died about four years ago, and my mother is in a nursing home right now.
> Interviewer: Nearby?
> Jim: No, down by B———, not too far. It's only an hour and fifteen minutes away. So I see her, but . . . to tell you personally, she's not in very good shape right now, so . . .
> Interviewer: It makes it difficult.
> Jim: We're expecting it, you know, her to die . . . we all know what's happening, and she wants it that way, so . . .

Here we see how the personal and professional intersect and, hence, we begin to get some sense of the way the trajectory of the project collided with the trajectory of Jim's life. An alternative categorization was beginning to emerge. Perhaps Jim was telling the truth when he kept saying, "I'll get to it in the end." This did seem, after all, to be a tough time in his life—burying his dad, immersed in his mother's final illness, turning fifty. We began to view it as almost heroic that he would even attempt a major new undertaking under such circumstances: Jim's forthrightness seemed suddenly stoic, and many of our own conclusions seemed painfully inadequate.

> Interviewer: Do you have any other comments about how the project's gone? Do you feel like you've gotten enough support from us at the Faculty?
> Jim: Yep, yep. I just haven't taken advantage of you, that's all. So it's—it's only one person to lay the blame on and that's me. I have—it's down there, it's waiting to go . . . Steve is willing to help and I've been the oversized elephant with lead in my feet. So it's up to me. It's not your fault, or [the

other researchers], or Steve's, or the school's, or anybody else's. It's me.
So, we're going to start next week. We're going to make the time.

In addition to learning more about Jim's personal life, we gradually learned
more about his teaching style, both from our own classroom observations
and from the other teachers. Our fieldnotes referred to another conversation with his department head:

> Steve then said something that may hold the key to Jim's reluctance to get
> involved: he said that Jim is a very well-prepared teacher, who always spends
> a great deal of time getting ready for each class. Steve said that Jim keeps
> careful records of previous lesson plans and exams, and consults them fre-
> quently. He has seen Jim completely replicate a handout for a class by re-
> writing it, even though it could be simply reproduced from the older
> documents.

Meanwhile, in the last semester of the project's data gathering, Jim had finally begun, in his own time, to take up computers—after two years of "resistance," and as the project neared its end. Late fieldnotes recounted a trip
through Jim's school:

> I started the day in the computer lab, where Jim was once again. While start-
> ing later than the others, he seems to be going full steam ahead with the
> computers. He has had both classes in three times already, and has the lab
> booked for periods 1 and 5 . . . on the following dates: November 22, 23,
> 27, 29, 30 and December 3. He was busy printing copies of maps in the lab
> for use with upcoming projects.

The new sensitivities we developed by means of the life history conversations with Jim began to be reflected in our accounts of events:

> Jim, having "lost his virginity" with the computers, now cannot get enough.
> He has booked his classes into the lab for 6 of 8 days. To some extent, this
> appears to be an imitation of Steve's exercise for OAC [senior academic] stu-
> dents. However, I also believe it has to do with the whole rationale for Jim's
> reluctance to date. He did not want to use the computers just to do some
> sort of half-assed exercise; if he was going to use them, he wanted it to be a
> serious data analysis problem. He has now jumped in at the deep end, and
> is doing a great deal with the system all at once. He is having problems, but
> coping with them pretty well.

Thus, by moving beyond the easy stereotyping of Jim, and sticking with
our methodological commitments, we were eventually able to develop a

fuller and more accurate picture of what his participation meant to an understanding of the innovation under study. By listening to his colleagues' characterizations, but refraining from joining in on them too quickly, we were able to delve below the surface impression of Jim as a "problem case" for the implementation of computers in his school. We might have settled for a perception of Jim's reluctance as a technical difficulty for staff training and implementation efforts. Instead, we drew upon his life history, and worked to establish a rapport with him, in order to allow us to see the introduction of new technology as he saw it. What emerged was a picture of a teacher in late maturity who had his own set of problems to deal with, but who also had clear commitments to his own standards of teaching, and clear ideas as to how he was going to go about incorporating new technologies into his practice. We began to understand that Jim was willing to use his seniority and his tenure to resist the bullying that often accompanies imposed innovation. By remaining open to alternative interpretations, we not only gained a different picture of Jim; we eventually saw him come to the technology, in his own time and on his own terms.

Concluding Remarks

This individual study of the culture clash between a subject teacher and newly introduced computer technology suggests a number of key questions for those studying new technologies "in the heat of the moment."

Centrally, the study should pose questions about the kind of research methodologies that we employ in our studies. All too often, our methodologies conspire with a narrow conception of the possibilities and problems of technical implementation. This technical focus is widely underwritten by those change and reform models that develop a technical vision of how to deliver "effective schools." But changing schooling is not, above all, a question of technical fine tuning, but of personal and cultural adaptation. The technical change agent and technically oriented researcher tend to narrow our vision to that which is technically achievable. The result is a vision that is socially parsimonious and essentially conservative. Without cultural change and an associated cultural vision, little can be achieved in terms of educational or broader social change. That, of course, may be the point, but why as researchers should we join in such a technical and impoverished enterprise?

Our task then is to develop modes of research that reassert a focus on the cultural and personal, and on what we call the "personality of change" (Goodson 2001). In this way, we might come to understand more about the culture clashes that inevitably underpin technical change processes. Most importantly, we may come to understand the broader balance between teachers' personal missions and identity projects, and attempts at educational change, such as the introduction of computers. By broadening our research page, we raise issues about the current wave of educational reforms that link the personal to the political—in this case, linking the imposition of new information technologies to individual "technologies of the self." In insisting on this research focus, we hope to salvage a concern with the cultural and personal from the bankrupt language of technical implementation and performance, into which studies of change within Western societies have unfortunately been increasingly cast.

3

DOWNSIZING THE WATERSHED

WITHIN THE FRAMEWORK LAID OUT IN CHAPTER 1, this chapter aims to assess some of the fruitful possibilities, and some of the dangers, that await the users of educational technology. The research reported here was conducted in southwestern Ontario, Canada, and centered primarily on the development and implementation of an integrated digital information system that was known variously as *The Watershed Information System, Map-Connections,* or *Point of View.* We shall refer to this system as The Watershed Information System, or just The Watershed for short.

The Watershed was not another instance of the imposition from above of government-developed curriculum and technology (as was discussed in chapter 2). Instead, it was privately developed, produced, and promoted. It embodied, we believe, some genuinely fresh and innovative thinking—both in terms of the technological applications involved and the context in which they were positioned. Despite such positive qualities, The Watershed struggled to define for itself a new space within the Ontario school system. In some ways, the difficulties that beset The Watershed re-enacted a classic pattern of educational innovation and resistance; in other ways, they speak to the current social and political context of ICT implementation in schools in unanticipated ways.

For us, technology-based innovations like The Watershed present important potential for reshaping schools in the twenty-first century. Paradoxically, however—as we will discuss in this chapter—such innovations also appear to face a range of complex hurdles, both within the context of schooling and within the larger social and political milieu. For our assessment of The Watershed we have employed a theoretical framework based on the work of Joseph Schwab (see Schwab, Jackson, Westbury, and Wilkof 1978) and developed by William Reid (1992; 1999) and others:

the "commonplaces of curriculum." Consistent with the metaphor of mapping and claiming spaces that has organized much of our discussion so far, Reid identifies five "common places," which he defines as "generally agreed-upon *places* where we should search" (Reid 1999, p. 202) for clues to understanding curricular phenomena. These are the *teacher*, the *student*, the *subject matter*, the *milieux*, and the process of *curriculum making*. All of these commonplaces have some import for understanding the evolution of The Watershed system. We will start by situating the system within its various milieux, and then move into the more particular commonplaces from there.

The Context of Innovation in Ontario

The global milieu in which The Watershed arose was described to some extent in chapter 1. It was a milieu shaped by the rapid and enormous growth of new digital and educational technologies that began in the late 1970s and continues still, and by the government-backed integration of these new technologies into classroom teaching. Within this milieu, the increase in the use of digital information and communication technologies specifically—computers and their communications networks—has been particularly remarkable (see OTA 1995). Growing access to the internet and the World Wide Web has provided an explosion of information resources for teachers and students.

Despite this pattern of growth, however, and as discussed in the previous chapter, these new ICTs are used by many teachers as "just another tool," with little fundamental impact on their basic pedagogical practices (Goodson and Mangan 1995b; Lankshear 1997; Lankshear and Bigum 2000). Many educators who use new technologies have not taken full advantage of the possibilities they present for restructuring curriculum and pedagogy. As Michael Hannafin noted in 1992, "Advances in computers and related hardware technologies have far out-stripped prevailing [instructional] design methodologies. The field remains insulated from developments of considerable consequence for improving learning" (p. 49). However, it must also be acknowledged that there is a growing body of theory and practice that incorporates constructivist learning theory and collaborative curriculum designs into technology-rich classroom environments (see Adams and Hamm 1996; Koschmann 1996). Canada has been a primary site for some of these developments (see Harasim 1995; Scardamalia and Bereiter 1996).

What is peculiar about this situation is that, even though the research and development milieu is complex and even paradoxical, and the implementation of ICTs uneven, the policy milieu has been strikingly uniform.

Throughout the English-speaking world, and in North America in particular, government policy regarding the computerization of education has been uncritically enthusiastic for decades. In the United States, getting schools "wired" became such a priority for the Clinton administration that the topic appeared in several State of the Union addresses (e.g., Clinton 1994; 1996; 1997). In the United Kingdom, as we discuss in chapter 6, the introduction of ICTs into schools has been a vast national project whose rationale has been rhetorically tied to enhanced academic achievement and international competitiveness (see Blair 1997; 1999). Indeed, there has been surprisingly little partisan debate over the benefits of computerizing schools. To some extent this silence may be attributable to the significant monetary paybacks for private industry involved in the push to get new digital technologies into schools, and to the fact that computerization often works to reinforce bureaucratic control of curriculum (Mangan 1994).

Parallel to the growing government emphasis on digital technologies has been a renewed emphasis on integrating curriculum subject areas. To some extent, this may be nothing more than one of those pendulum swings in curriculum policy and practice that vacillate between creating new subject boundaries and tearing down old ones (Goodson 1985). It may also, however, reflect a neo-liberal interest in having schools serve more closely the interests of the "real world" of work, in which academic distinctions are seen as largely irrelevant (see Gee, Hull, and Lankshear 1996, Robertson 1998). In Ontario, these parallel trends were highlighted when a mid-1990s Royal Commission reinforced earlier government policy statements and strongly supported both integrated approaches to curriculum and expanded use of information technologies (Ont. RCoL 1995; Ont. Min. of Ed. 1995). Yet despite policy and infrastructure investment in new ICTs on the government's part, the 1995 Royal Commission also reported that much of the potential of this new educational technology was as yet poorly developed and little understood.

In Canada, where provincial governments still hold the balance of power in important areas such as health care and education policy, this Royal Commission report experienced a fate similar to many others: it caused a certain number of ripples and a couple of potentially significant changes, but was largely ignored in those areas where politicians chose to do so. The Commission had been established by a social-democratic government, but shortly after its report was issued, a conservative government was elected. That government brought with it a very different social agenda, a very different attitude toward schools, and—perhaps most far-reaching in terms of impact—a clear animus toward the province's unionized teachers. A stunningly rapid set of reforms was instituted in the late

1990s, including an entire new curriculum, re-centralized administration of economic and organizational decisions, and a number of measures designed to reinforce control of teachers' work. These included the establishment of a College of Teachers with new disciplinary powers, the institution of standardized tests for teacher certification, and legislation specifying (and increasing) the exact number of minutes teachers were to spend in classrooms each week (Ont. Ed. Act 170.2[1]). These reforms were considered draconian by many teachers, and were actively resisted in many cases, culminating in a province-wide walkout by the union in the fall of 1997 (Smaller 1998). In general, however, such acts of resistance were futile. The result was that throughout the period from 1997 to 2001, Ontario teachers (especially in high schools) were faced with a series of new demands that placed them under a great deal of stress. As we shall see, this political and organizational context had a great deal to do with the prospects of The Watershed as a curricular innovation.

The Software Application and its Curriculum Connections

The Watershed Information System was intended to be a response to some of the challenges of using digital information and communication technologies in new ways, and of developing curricular activities that would be both integrated and integrative. That is, the goal underpinning its design was the involvement of activities from a number of disciplines, and the curriculum developed to accompany the technology was designed to encourage students to become involved with their school, their local community, and the rest of the province (and the world) in novel ways.

The Watershed was originally conceived by architect and environmentalist Fred McGarry and his colleagues. It was designed and implemented by a team of university professors and researchers, private software developers, business sponsors, and teachers and students in the high schools of the Grand River Watershed, in and around Cambridge, Ontario. It is unquestionably much more than just another piece of educational software. The Watershed was designed to challenge not only traditional forms of curriculum and pedagogy, but a plethora of traditional educational relationships: relationships between schools and their communities; between vendors and consumers; between the producers of information and the end-users; between subject areas within the school; and between teachers and students. The project, then, did not lack for imagination or forward thinking. However, the scope of innovation that was being attempted subjected the project to unforeseen problems and forms of resistance from many different directions.

Reid's "commonplace" of subject matter provides us with a useful launching pad for discussing the actual content of The Watershed Information System. From this vantage point, the fundamental ideas behind the software application are seen readily as cross-curricular and integrative in nature, but with an emphasis on geography—a discipline that itself takes pride in integrating a variety of sub-disciplinary forms of knowledge (Goodson 1992a). Content was deliberately designed to offer a wide variety of important information that could be indexed and accessed by means of an object-oriented "clickable" map of the area in which a participating school was located. The oft-cited metaphor of "mapping information" was to be taken literally within The Watershed system and its multi-layered database of economic, demographic, and environmental information. The database was hyperlinked to finely detailed digital maps of a given area (generated using the conventions of a Geographical Information System, or GIS). Users could point-and-click on various parts of the map to call up information about the natural features, buildings, history, and demographics of the region.

The educational uses of such a detailed database, as envisioned by the developers, would be many and varied. Students could explore local history, genealogy, economic development, and environmental change. Moreover, the envisaged educational applications of The Watershed were not limited to its use as a databank for information "withdrawals." The students were also expected to make important deposits by creating and maintaining the various databases. In other words, the developers' intention was that the neighbourhood databases would be updated and expanded continuously by the users themselves. To a significant extent, this vision was realized during the early implementation of the system, as class projects were developed to regularly update the system's databases. One class project, for example, included mapping a local cemetery. For each headstone, the epitaph was recorded as text, a video image of the stone was captured, and the precise location was determined using surveying techniques. All of these data were then incorporated into the on-line database. Learning outcomes accrued as a result of this particular project included a greater appreciation of important historical artifacts of the local area, as well as presenting students with "real-life" opportunities to apply mathematics, media studies, English, historiography, and computer-science skills within the context of a project that was meaningful to the students (Pollock-Ellwand 1998). Teachers involved with this and similar projects reported such high enthusiasm among students that many worked on Watershed-related projects during after-school hours, and even after classes had ended for the summer.

Another important dimension of The Watershed Information System was the way it promoted interaction between each participating school and its surrounding community. When fully developed, Watershed databases were designed to be accessible to anybody in the community. Individual citizens who wished to research their family history or the context of a heritage building site, for example, would be able to do so by accessing relevant Watershed databases from any internet-connected computer. Moreover, existing community resources, such as those produced independently by oral historians or housed within private memorabilia collections, were subsequently incorporated into "neighborhood databases" within The Watershed system.

A number of curriculum-development projects were launched concomitantly with software development. These projects were designed deliberately to make explicit, practical bridges between The Watershed and the prescribed curriculum of Ontario. Initially, these projects were designed and implemented by volunteer teachers in concert with program developers. As the project began to struggle, the developers hired a professional curriculum consultant to come up with lesson plans linked to the provincial curriculum (see Point of View 2000).

In addition to technical and curricular initiatives, The Watershed had several important and innovative "off-line" aspects to it. For instance, although there was already in existence a list of software approved by the Ministry of Education for use in schools, McGarry and his associates decided not to seek this form of official approval. Instead, they chose to work directly with local schools and teachers to develop curriculum resources to be used with Watershed. Rather than seek provincial subsidies for schools to buy their product, the developers set out to craft "partnerships" between schools and businesses by finding corporate sponsors to pay for the installation of the software within each school.

Although their approach involved a good deal of extra sales effort on the part of the developers, it reaped some immediate benefits. Not the least among these was the fact that only those teachers and schools that exhibited enthusiasm and commitment to the project became involved in the initiative. This effectively avoided the need to convince reluctant participants to join the effort, or having to deal with their resistance during implementation. To some extent, this approach was successful, especially in the early stages of the project. Demonstrations of the prototype software were held at a number of high schools in the Kitchener-Waterloo-Cambridge area, and several of them, primarily in the smaller, more rural communities of the region, signed on as eager participants.

The Copper Trust and the On-line Academy

A further innovative aspect of The Watershed Information System was that the entire effort was supposed to be financed through a non-profit trust that sponsored an "on-line academy." The Copper Trust was a registered non-profit corporation established by the developers of The Watershed. Their intention was that eventually the development of the software and associated curricular material would be undertaken collectively by members of the trust, that is, the schools who subscribed to the system. The stated goals of the Copper Trust were to provide:

> comprehensive support for curriculum resources development by teachers, using the *Point Of View* model and an on-line peer information sharing system. Through an on-line E-Zine forum that includes editorial comment and discussion, peer review, workshops, face-to-face sessions, and best practice awards, the Learning Innovation Service will support the development of new curriculum resources generated from teacher's initiatives in the classroom and the community. These new curriculum resources will then be used to augment the Academy's Current Teachers Resources database. (Point of View 2000)

Although the applications developed within the context of the On-line Academy were geared to the official Ontario curriculum, there was also a clear intent to replicate The Watershed model by building up a corpus of users who would develop and share their own resources outside of the official guidelines and other curriculum documents.

The On-line Academy, other key features of the Copper Trust, and The Watershed system in general, could be seen as "counter-hegemonic," as least in comparison with the usual proprietary concerns of private developers and the official education system in Ontario. The contents of the student-built databases were intended to be publicly accessible, and owned in common by all participants through their membership in the Copper Trust. Once the developers accomplished the basic implementation of The Watershed, further development was to be conducted by using the telecommunications capabilities of the network to conduct ongoing dialogues and online "town hall" meetings among student and community participants. It was intended that students, teachers, and private users would all have equal input to these discussions. The On-line Academy would also supervise annual awards recognizing "best practices" in using the system. These "academy awards" would be given based on feedback from all participants, and were intended to foster a sense of pride among those involved (ibid.).

The development and marketing of The Watershed thus came close to embodying some of the novel features of the new information economy discussed in chapter 1. To the extent that the developers expected to profit from bringing the product to market, they saw their income being generated by the initial funding of the project and its sale to schools, supported by corporate donations. Once the system was in place throughout the province (and possibly throughout Canada or even the world), it was to be turned over to the jointly managed Copper Trust, after which its further growth would be in the hands of its users.

The Vision Meets the Realities of Schooling

From the descriptions presented so far, it should be clear that The Watershed concept did not lack for vision. Not only was it an innovative software concept at the time, but the entire nexus of relationships around that concept had been re-thought. From the way the software was developed and financed, to the ways in which participants were recruited and funded, to the curriculum concepts underlying the project, and on into the kinds of sustaining relationships that were to be encouraged and supported, almost everything about the project had a different "shape" and "quality" compared to more traditional curriculum development efforts. The developers seemed to have faith that this revolutionary approach would enable them to succeed where others before them had had little impact (the government-sponsored ICON system being perhaps the most disastrous example; see Mangan 1994).

Unfortunately, and despite the developers' and participants' best efforts, a number of pitfalls awaited The Watershed project that dealt it a series of heavy blows during its first two to three years. As we learned by interviewing the developers, their curriculum consultants, and participating teachers, the challenges that faced The Watershed were often similar to those facing other educational ICT innovations. They included technical problems of hardware and software availability and training; finance; integration with existing curricula; and the organizational pressures arising from the current wave of school restructuring. In addition to these predictable problems, however, the developers had to educate potential clients and sponsors about various aspects of their innovative approach, as described above. Paradoxically, then, the very aspects of The Watershed that aroused enthusiasm among some teachers also created unusual hurdles for its incorporation into Ontario schools, and eventually stunted its growth. Its main legacy may be to serve as yet another example of the friction produced between innovative ideas and the various forms of inertia and resistance within the established school system.

In the remainder of this chapter we will further examine the fate of The Watershed, using the lenses of the commonplaces of curriculum, and drawing primarily on interview data collected from participants in some of the early installations. The names of cooperating schools and teachers have been replaced by pseudonyms to protect the confidentiality of the informants.

The Technical Milieu

It may not be surprising to educators who are familiar with information technologies to discover that the technical resources required by a project like The Watershed often outstripped what was available in schools, especially those in smaller communities. In these excerpts from interviews, "Lauren" is a social studies teacher who was working in the small community of "Wexford." "Lynn" is a history and English teacher and "Bill" is a mathematics teacher, both from the larger town of "Denton." "Barney" is a computer-science teacher from the village of "Frostburg."

> Interviewer: Did you have the sense that the software required some pretty sophisticated hardware to run? Did it actually require that it have its own computer dedicated to it?
>
> Lauren: . . . I think this computer essentially worked as a server for the program. And because we didn't want to put it on at that time, they were working through the University of Waterloo's computer bank, so I think the computer we had was kind of the intermediary. We could take, I put information on disks, and then on that computer, and then that computer kind of sorted things before it went to the main server for *Map-Connections* at the time. So, that has probably all changed since we originally put it on. Was it as sophisticated? It was more sophisticated than what we were working with in individual classrooms—not necessarily the computer labs. It was, it was the stuff above what the school system was having, but you could still use what the school system had to produce the materials—the content. But you had to have this one machine to work with.

❏ ❏ ❏ ❏ ❏

> Lynn: I've never used it, because it won't go on our school network, and my home computer is not powerful enough to run it without a lot of help from someone else.
>
> Interviewer: So it is a pretty, kind of, demanding piece of software, then?
>
> Lynn: Yeah, well, you couldn't put it on the network, and you see, that's what we have, and if it's just on a stand-alone computer, it's not terribly useful for a class.
>
> Interviewer: Right. So, is it meant to run on the local area network, or is it meant to actually use the World Wide Web?
>
> Lynn: I think it's meant to—the material you're publishing—is meant to go on the World Wide Web. But you have to have something to work on it, to set up the web pages.

> Interviewer: So the hardware and the software never got together while you were at Denton?
>
> Lynn: No. Now, we may have individual stand-alones that are powerful enough to run it, but um. . . . I think there's a new map that came out in the final version, which I haven't seen, but the first map took almost an hour to download.

The software was demanding, then, and it was also not completely bug-free.

> Barney: It was all sort of Beta software at first, and not everything worked right. It was a long process to improve the software, and one of the ways they did it was by having people interact with it. So as we tried using the software to do things, we would say, "well, it doesn't do this or it doesn't do that," or "it's very cumbersome" or complicated. They would go back and try to make improvements. So it was an ongoing, sort of back-and-forth game of leapfrog.
>
> First of all, everything was based on the map. So the person would have to go online, go to the *Point of View* site, and then they would have to download the map to their computer. Once the map was downloaded, then they could access the information on the map. The point-and-click was on the map. So you would click on something on the map, and if there was information in the database associated with what you clicked on the map, it would then go and get the information from the site, and put it up on your computer screen. So it was this two-step process, where you had to first put the map on your machine, and then once you had the map, then you could access the information in the database. So it was pretty cumbersome.

The problems with the map signaled in these excerpts refer to the complexity of the graphical user interface settled upon for the maps within The Watershed software. In order to achieve the level of detail wanted by the developers, simple graphic maps were not enough. Instead, fully digital databases in the format required by Geographical Information Systems (GIS) were required, and these constituted huge files by the standards of most home and school computer systems. It would appear, then, that the developers, who were used to working with powerful systems of their own, overestimated either the level of computing power available in most schools, or their ability to convince corporate and community sponsors to supply the required state-of-the-art equipment. The result was that the system never became fully operational at any of the schools where it was installed.

The other clear impression from the quotations above is that the technical details of the software and hardware configurations were only understood by most teachers in a general, indeed a fairly fuzzy, sort of way. The teachers all reported that their teaching priorities were connected to using the software, not to installing and maintaining it. Paradoxically, this lack of concern with the technical side of operating and managing the program may have impeded its full implementation and use in schools.

The Financial Milieu

Related to the issue of sophisticated hardware and software and teachers' priorities was the expense involved in the project. As mentioned earlier, the original plan was that no funding would be required from the provincial Ministry of Education, or from the local school district. Instead, each school was to be partnered with a corporate sponsor who would in turn reap some free good-will publicity from making a contribution in cash or in kind. However, this plan also ran into problems.

> Interviewer: Were there corporate sponsors involved, and did they buy hardware as well as the software for the school? Or did you use the school's own computers?
>
> Lauren: At one of these points Hereford had a seventy-fifth school anniversary, and we made some money, so some money from that was devoted to the computer. Um, computer or software, one of those we never did pay for. . . . We did have some donations from local corporate sponsors—not a lot I don't think—but I think most of them came from this fundraising that we had. And I'm not exactly sure how that money was disbursed. But we did end up with a dedicated computer which was high-end enough. And we had lots of problems getting the internet connections and whatever, just because the school didn't have them all. So we had to get all that in, too.

❐ ❐ ❐ ❐ ❐

> Lynn: We had interest and support, but not connected to any money. So I think it all came from our school, but I may be wrong about that.
>
> Interviewer: Really? Oh. So there wasn't a big announcement of a corporate sponsor at some point?
>
> Lynn: I think the principal and Fred and several others went around and made various presentations, but I don't think we got a corporate sponsor.

Thus, despite a good deal of rhetoric from the Ontario Ministry of Education about the importance and desirability of such partnerships, none of these schools was able to locate a sponsor who was actually willing to invest in the project. The developers' slightly maverick attitude may in fact have hurt them here, because it might have been easier to locate such a sponsor with some government help. Whatever the cause, however, the project found itself looking for significant financing in a time when governments were cutting back and consolidating, and when locally oriented, smaller businesses were reluctant to commit their own funds. In most cases it was left up to the schools themselves to come up with funding.

The Institutional Milieu

Alongside difficulties in securing financing faced by participating schools, another issue emerged around establishing secure bases of personnel. A project as complex as The Watershed, which aims to recruit teachers directly, must rely on teachers being in one place and involved in the project for an extended period of time. The failure to establish and maintain such a personnel base proved to be a major impediment to the successful, widespread implementation of The Watershed.

As we mentioned earlier, Ontario's provincial government began in 1999 to impose new curricula for almost every subject at every grade level. These reforms came on top of other initiatives in the late 1990s. The government legislated increased teaching time, and new schemes for guiding and advising students (see Ont. Min. of Ed. 1998; 1999). The new demands were combined with decreases in specialized support staff, amalgamations of school districts, generally dwindling budgets, and the elimination of a fifth year of high school (which had been in place for over forty years). The subsequent increased work burden on teachers led to massive numbers of early retirements and escalating forms of resistance among teachers. As well as the month-long walkout in 1997, the 1999 to 2000 school year saw many teachers' unions staging work-to-rule campaigns, or withdrawing support for extracurricular activities.

As a direct result of these conditions it seems, teachers in Ontario became much more mobile than previously. As older teachers retired, those that remained sought to find placements that were more convenient, and/or that would minimize their extra work and responsibility loads. Barney described this process, and identified it explicitly as a factor undermining the effectiveness of the project:

> Well, the principal retired. The other two staff members, each was head of a department. And within this board, due to cuts, department headships were decimated in many ways. They've lost their time, they've lost almost all of their money. So I think perhaps that was one small part of the fact that both of these ladies left. But the other thing was that neither of them lived in this area. They both lived in the Cambridge area. And as a result, I think that when opportunities arose to move closer to home and teach

closer to home, they decided that things are better there than they are here, so they both decided to make the move, I guess. But it really did affect the whole program here.

The effects of increased workloads and the loss of support networks were also reported. When asked whether he was still using this software in any of his classes, Barney replied:

> I have not used it this year. Really, I haven't even looked at it since I came back in September [2000]. I started back in September doing my four out of four right off the bat. I don't know if that's a good reason for not doing anything, but I was pretty swamped for the first two and half months, just trying to keep my head above water, teaching four classes a day. But the people who spearheaded this whole thing were all gone. The people that were gathering the information, that were saying, "Come on, Barney, let's go to this workshop," so I'd go along with them, those three people in particular were spearheading everything. . . . And although I truly thought it was a very good idea, it wasn't something I was ready to pick the ball up and run with by myself.

As we saw in "Jim's" case in chapter 2, the factors impacting Barney's personal life, and the lives of his co-workers, began to overwhelm their interest and enthusiasm for the technological innovation. A similar pattern was revealed by an e-mail received from a teacher who had been one of the most enthusiastic participants in The Watershed project. He had left the school where he had helped establish The Watershed, to become a vice-principal at another high school in a different area. When contacted at his new school, he replied with the following e-mail:

Subject: Re: Research?
Date: Thu, 25 Jan 2001 18:04:53 −0500
From: Bill_Masters

Hi there!!!
    Since last year I've changed jobs . . . I'm now VP at Mead High School . . . and I'm not quite overwhelmed (but I'm at least "whelmed") . . . so I haven't done anything to further the projects that I was involved in. At Denton Collegiate, four "key players" have evaporated . . . myself . . . a computer tech teacher (gave birth to a boy yesterday) . . . a geographer (on a planned leave of absence) . . . and a scientist (seconded by a publisher to bail out the writing of a grade eleven text). . . .
    So I don't even know who to refer you to . . . my HOPE was to foster some of the kinds of things that we undertook at DCI here at my new school, but I seem to be dealing more with the ne'r do wells and malcontents

than things pedagogical. . . . As I watch what's coming from the Ministry most recently (the Exemplars Project . . . where samples of student work are held up to the scrutiny of the charts of expectations for each new secondary course), it does fold nicely into the paradigm of the "living book" that we had a vision of. . . . In the work that we did, students would use as a model the work of previous classes of students . . . they would build upon and re-fine the previous students' work, using that older work as a model. In a sim-ilar way, the Exemplars Project uses previous students' work to help establish the quality of more recent work . . . I think there's a good idea in here, but neither the time nor the personnel exist for further pursuit!!!

Cheers, eh?
Bill

The need for continuity is clearly expressed here, but it is just as clearly frustrated by the circumstances surrounding the school. Lynn summarized the situation succinctly:

> It almost needs a consistent teacher over a number of years, working on ironing out the bugs as you go along. And that again, I think, is increasingly one of the difficulties. I don't know whether that's going to be as possible in the future, in the next few years, as it's been in the past.

Lauren and Barney expressed the ways in which the technical problems and the other sources of stress came together for teachers in classrooms:

> Lauren: I'm extremely frustrated with how slow the computers got, and the computer programs etcetera. . . . What we were going to do was put some sample recipes on the website. Well, by the time you get them and format them and type them and proof them and, you know, all those stages were frustrating. . . . And then, we've just been downloaded so much more in the last years it's difficult to do. I thought, you know, "Oh, this is great. I can go!" Well, you can't get there that fast.

❒ ❒ ❒ ❒ ❒

> Barney: I thought, this is a wonderful idea. It's just the implementation—the time, the effort, the lack of resources. I thought this was great. It combined local information, meaningful information, into the cur-riculum. And then the idea of being able to publish it eventually onto the internet so that anyone could see it. People, students could then see their work. I thought that was great. And I still think it's a great idea. It's just that no-one seems to have the time or the resources to make use of it at this point in time. . . . And the people who spear-headed it in the school, when all three left at the same time, it really left a void here.

The teachers themselves, then, seemed well aware of the ways in which Ministry restructuring programs affected their everyday practice, and the general conditions of their work. Nonetheless, even though The Watershed had its roots in a time before the current government came to office, the people who developed The Watershed were aware of the permanent state of tension between teachers and their political masters. This was one reason why they chose deliberately to work outside of the official regulatory framework, and to take advantage of the scant opportunities remaining for teachers to exercise their discretion and their academic freedom in deciding on curricular tools. However, the combination of the technical, financial, and institutional milieux in which The Watershed was implemented worked to undermine the potential for success of the initiative.

We are thus led from our consideration of the various milieux of this innovation back to the everyday realities of the classroom. By looking at the commonplaces of teachers and students, we will see where The Watershed has achieved some partial successes, despite the many problems it has confronted.

The Watershed in Practice:
Students and Teachers

Despite the difficulties that teachers encountered during the implementation of The Watershed, they remained surprisingly upbeat about the project. The interview data we collected strongly suggest that, far from finding the experience full of frustration and failure, participants found the project to be exciting and challenging in positive ways, and pleasingly innovative.

Notwithstanding all of the technical difficulties, many participating teachers reported that they and their students actually reaped some of the intended rewards of the system. They spoke of greater cross-curricular integration, greater community involvement, and improved motivation for students, derived from participating in a real data-gathering effort with public results.

> Interviewer: So it sounds like some of these technical problems were a big disappointment. Do you think it was still kind of a learning experience, though?
>
> Lynn: Oh yeah. . . . It was a *really* exciting project. I'm just so glad I got involved with it. It was disappointing that I never got the stuff on the internet, but the bottom line for me was, the kids did some really neat research. Over the three years I was working on it, I think we interviewed—let's see—almost forty people, and those transcripts are stored at the [town] Archives. And so, it was a collaboration with the Archives and the school that really was very beneficial to both. It was exciting to

see the involvement of the kids. The first year I did it, there were kids who came in after school to finish working on the school computers, to get the transcripts worked out. I tried to make them realize that they were making a commitment, not only to the school project, but also to people in the community. And they had to finish it.

Lauren and Barney had some similar experiences:

> Interviewer: One of the real innovative thrusts of this idea as I understood it was to encourage collaboration across subject areas and so forth. Did that happen in your school, and how?
>
> Lauren: Yeah, yeah, you know it just goes on and on and on. One year we did marketing, we had the local blueberry growers come in. . . . So, they came in, presented their information to my marketing class, my marketing class then took that and they were to create a pamphlet, web pages, information about them. We took that information, gave it to the computing class, and they typed it up and they generated pamphlets and information from that. And then this—some of this—was to go into *MapConnections.* . . . Roy was basically computers, so anytime we had data he inputted it that way. Carolyn . . . I think she had the grade eleven media class do the web pages. Took those web pages to the senior classes and had them peer-edit them. . . . So lots of integration. But that was really easy in a small school. . . . In Wexford it was just the set-up of the school. . . . we all ate in the same lunch room. Every teacher at Wexford knew about *MapConnections.* They may have not had actual input into it but I know the geography class mapped the working cemetery. You know, we did the pioneer, which was the old one, and the geography class used it to map the newer cemetery. Now I don't know how much of that got *onto MapConnections,* but they did that *because* of *MapConnections.* And the art class got involved in the historical society and built heritage. . . . So almost every department got involved in some way or was able to be involved.

❑ ❑ ❑ ❑ ❑

> Interviewer: And do you think that the students appreciated this cross-curricular integration notion, that, you know, there were different aspects to this and they could work on it in different classes?
>
> Lauren: I certainly think my students did, but again I think it takes somebody who's keen and sees the connections, to reinforce that with the kids. . . . We didn't start it off in grade nine, just because of the—what the curriculum has, but grade tens and elevens were probably the ones who were most active. And then you get independent studies and some of those kids would ask to do ISUs [Independent Study Units] using *MapConnections,* and some of the materials they did before, you know? "I did a web page last year. Well, could I not take this and refine it?" So, they did a cross-curricular unit themselves in many cases.

□ □ □ □ □

Barney: The one thing I always liked about *Point of View* was the idea. It was a great idea. It really made a lot of sense. . . . Whether it's taking pictures of the cemetery. . . . If you can integrate it into the curriculum, so much the better. If they can publish that to the internet, it's got benefits for the community. When we were selling this to the community as a whole, I would talk just like that.

Statements such as these raise interesting contrasts with the rest of the world of educational technology. There are hundreds of companies hawking products that promise an education revolution and more. But many of these products fail to deliver on their inflated claims, as Barney attested:

I bought all this wonderful educational software. And I spent hundreds and hundreds of hours testing it, trying it, to see where I could fit this into the classroom. And what I realized was that it was all inadequate. Like yeah, I could use this for ten minutes in the classroom, or fifteen minutes in the classroom. . . . But you have to spend so many hours finding something that you could use for fifteen minutes at a certain point in the year, that it all became too time-consuming.

Ironically, when so much hype surrounds so many educational technologies that actually deliver so little, The Watershed, with less publicity and more modest claims, achieved some of its pedagogical goals despite the problems and pitfalls it encountered along the way.

Conclusion

At the time of writing, the story of The Watershed was not yet over. The developers and a few enthusiastic teachers and principals were still seeking to expand the number of installations and applications of the system. But the history of the project suggests that this enthusiasm will still encounter many of the same constraints that have faced other efforts to reform and restructure schooling. There is room for innovation, but there are also powerful forces working to reproduce and reinforce the power relations and institutional arrangements that have been in place for decades. Against this background, there are a number of important lessons that can be learned from the current outcomes of this project.

Perhaps the first and most important lesson is that there are imaginative and creative educators at work who are committed to developing new visions of integrative curriculum employing information and communications technologies. The possibilities presented by projects that incorporate access to comprehensive local databases and global connections by means of new and emerging ICTs are more fruitful than some critics may imagine. Nevertheless, the development of these possibilities and potentials must still take place within school systems that have not only shown themselves to be remarkably resistant to change at times, but that are also subject to both old and new constraints.

Scrutinizing the commonplaces of "curriculum making" reveals many familiar, and some not-so-familiar, barriers to genuinely new forms of technology-rich instruction. Among the familiar constraints is funding, which is almost never adequate to satisfy many educators. However, in Ontario under a Conservative government, it has been particularly difficult to obtain funding from either public or private sectors. As the participating teachers pointed out, the lack of funding had many negative effects on the progress of The Watershed. The kind of computing power required to maximize the efficacy of a system as complex as The Watershed is expensive, and thus was not readily available to many schools—despite the glitter of a few showcase examples eagerly promoted by business and government. The other familiar constraints of infrastructure (internet wiring and lab space, for instance), hardware compatibility, and difficulties of training and maintenance, were only exacerbated by the demands of this high-tech project.

New ICT applications such as The Watershed will always encounter complex interactions among the social, political, economic, institutional, and technical milieux that surround public schooling. These milieux often present formidable obstacles to any fundamental change, and can be expected to intrude even where participants are not acutely aware of them. But in an environment in which wholesale restructuring has been imposed by a government anxious to put its stamp on one of the central social technologies under its jurisdiction, the obstacles are heightened. In fin-de-siècle Ontario, decreased teacher morale, increased rates of retirement and mobility, escalating workloads, and wholesale revisions to curriculum conspired to create a milieu that was clearly antagonistic to innovative applications of ICTs. We can only speculate as to whether that antagonistic milieu was an intended or unintended consequence of other fiscal and educational policies. But the evidence suggests that, despite paying lip service to an interest in educational innovation, the Conservative government of the day had other priorities that ranked higher than the promotion of integrative curriculum.

Perhaps the lesson of The Watershed has been that, in at least some cases, the most important function of innovative applications of technology may lie in their role as catalysts. The fact that they are sometimes able to inspire enthusiasm and commitment where both are waning, that they may be able to re-energize dispirited teachers and catch the imagination of technologically oriented young people, may allow them to catalyze new commitments to liberating forms of learning. Indeed, it is instructive to note that many of the imaginative and nontraditional aspects of The Watershed project were implemented despite difficulties with the technology and the bureaucracy. Cross-curricular, community-related projects were launched at several schools. Teachers and students expressed enthusiasm and satisfaction with these projects, even if only a few found their way onto the internet for public access.

Somewhat surprisingly then, the most important effects of this technology-based innovation may not have been related directly to the technological application. It may turn out that the curricular and pedagogical goals that were designed to accompany the technological innovation prove to be the most important part of the project. And maybe that is as it should be.

4

MACHINES AND MINDSETS

Mindsets

THE CONCEPT OF "MINDSETS" WAS INTRODUCED briefly in chapter 1. This chapter will examine that concept in more detail and use it as a tool to explore a number of ICT innovations in Australian schools. One of the mindsets described earlier centered on using new technologies as tools to simply implement slightly modified versions of old, established curriculum approaches. This mindset, in fact, was the norm in a two-year study of attempts to introduce computing applications into literacy education in 20 Australian classrooms ranging from pre-school to Grade 12. The classrooms ranged over urban/rural, high/low socioeconomic status, and single-sex/mixed-sex varieties, from lower-elementary to upper-secondary levels (Lankshear et al. 1997, Vols. 1 and 2; Lankshear and Snyder 2000).

Almost entirely, the computer-mediated literacy activities observed in these schools involved long-established routine practices with computers being added on here and there. For example, word processing was used to produce final copies of work. Story writing, formulaic biographies, and story retellings were produced as slide shows or web pages. And the venerable "classroom newspaper" was used as a pretext for learning and using the columns function of word processing software. Similar results emerged from a study of Ontario high schools in the early 1990s, in which teachers repeatedly identified the new technology as "just another tool" to achieve their established purposes (Goodson and Mangan 1991; see also chapter 2 in this book).

While the use of drill-and-skill software for literacy acquisition did not figure largely in the sites investigated, it is a pervasive use of new technologies within literacy education throughout "advanced" Anglo-American school systems. There are, of course, some mitigating reasons for the "old wine in new bottles" syndrome. Many teachers have had little prior experience of and expertise with using computer applications for authentic everyday purposes (although this is becoming less common by the day). Even where official curriculum guidelines for using computers existed in the Australian study context, they reinforced conventional literacy practices and genres and, at best, invited imaginative incorporations of new technologies into familiar learning activities.

For example, in an Australian primary school with over 90 percent of its mixed-sex student population coming from non-English speaking backgrounds, Grade 2 students were observed using the two stand-alone computers (a Macintosh Performa 580CD and a Performa 400) in their classroom to facilitate their study of the narrative genre of stories. Genre-based learning figured strongly in the state's English language syllabus at the time, and the particular activities the students were engaged in involved pairs or groups producing multimedia presentations of stories (Lankshear 1998). In one activity they produced a story of their own. In others each pair produced jointly constructed retellings of a single page from *The Three Little Pigs* and *The Magic Flute*. Typical processes involved using multipanel storyboard formats on paper; roughing out ideas in pen, paper, and crayon; and then moving to drawing, painting, and sound applications on the computers to produce the final slides. As final outcomes, the individual pages were then assembled as slide-show presentations of the retold stories, using text, graphics, and sound. Despite the incorporation of new ICTs, the students were engaged in nothing more than highly structured read-and-retell practices found everywhere in primary schools prior to the flush of computers in classrooms.

These examples of established mindsets prevailing over new conditions can be contrasted with some of the insider mindsets proposed by some of the more forward-thinking theorists in the field. For example, an interesting and potentially useful way of thinking about many of the exemplars in the *Digital Rhetorics* project (Lankshear et al. 1997) was suggested by a set of three related distinctions drawn by John Perry Barlow (see Tunbridge 1995). These intimate a contemporary fracturing of "space" and a contemporary divergence in mindsets (Lankshear and Bigum 2000). Barlow's distinctions have to do with modes of controlling "goods" like values, morals, knowledge, competence, and the like. The way he frames and elucidates his distinctions may be seen as demarcating two broad mindsets: one that affirms the world as the same but just more technologized; the other that asserts that the world, because of the operation of these new technologies, is radically different.

Barlow's distinctions build on the idea of a fracturing of space between physical space and cyberspace. He sees these as fundamentally different kinds of spaces that operate according to different principles and procedures. Physical space is well known and understood and over millennia humans have developed laws, principles, and practices for living in this space. Cyberspace is new, however, and must be understood and approached in ways appropriate to it. Those who see the world as "the same as before, only more technologized" act out of a mindset that applies principles and procedures of physical ("industrial-era") space to cyberspace. Those who have "grown up" with cyberspace and know it from the inside do not approach it via principles and procedures of the physical space paradigm. They employ a different mindset.

Barlow's three distinctions are, briefly, as follows. First, he distinguishes the respective economies of the two spaces. In physical space, value is increased by regulating scarcity. To make a "good" more valuable one makes supply scarce (even though the "good" may, in fact, be quite abundant—like food, competence, or diamonds). Schools, for instance, have helped keep "competence" in scarce supply by credentialing achievement, and feeding into social constructions of "suitably" or "properly" credentialed attainment. By contrast, in the economy of cyberspace it is familiarity and dispersal, not scarcity, that has value. Information is a relationship rather than a commodity, and as with all relationships "the more that's going back and forth the higher the value of the relationship" (quoted in Tunbridge 1995, p. 4). In cyberspace, the more one tries to control the availability of information, the lower the value of that information because it is used, improved, and trafficked less.

The second distinction involves the ways issues and concerns in cyberspace are addressed. Some people try to tackle them (or even to instigate them) in ways that build on assumptions and principles associated with physical space. Barlow uses the examples of pornography on the net and Bill Gates's apparent maneuver to gain control of the internet by bundling *Microsoft Explorer* with *Windows 95/98*. There are very different ways of looking at these concerns depending on the mindset from which they are approached.

With respect to pornography on the net, Barlow rejects imposing gross filters. They can't work because net-space simply cannot be controlled in that way. The more elaborate the filter, the more elaborate the search to find ways around it, and the more powerful these resistances become. Barlow advocates applying more local and individualized filters that work on the principle of people taking responsibility for their choices and deciding what "noise" they want to filter out. This means that instead of trying to "weed out" pornography (or whatever) in order to shield children from it—which is impossible—caregivers should localize filters by educating their children to find it as distasteful as they do. Similarly, with the fear of Microsoft (or anyone) controlling net-space, the point is that the internet "is too complex for any one person or organization to create the software for it." Software development will continue to be organic, to be shared and dispersed. Short-term domains of control and influence will undoubtedly exist, but they cannot become total or monopolistic because of the very nature of the space.

Barlow's third distinction is between people who have been born into and have grown up in the context of cyberspace, on the one hand, and those who come to this new world from the standpoint of a life-long socialization in physical space, on the other. We will refer here to the former as "insiders" and the latter as "outsider-newcomers" (Barlow uses the term "natives" for insiders and "immigrants" for newcomers to cyberspace). This distinction marks off those who "understand the internet, virtual concepts and the IT world generally" from those who do not—that is, it distinguishes mindsets. Newcomers to cyberspace don't have the experiences, history, and resources available to them that insiders have, so they cannot understand the space in the ways that insiders do. Barlow believes this distinction falls very much along age lines. Generally speaking, people born before 1970 are outsider-newcomers. Conversely, people in first-world societies under the age of 30 are "closer to being [insiders] in terms of understanding what [the internet, virtual concepts, and the IT world] is, and having a real basic sense of it" (ibid.). Paradoxically, then, older people tend to be newcomers to cyberspace, while members of the younger generation are more likely to be "veterans."

Barlow's general idea has many points of connection with current thinking. It resonates with Don Tapscott's (1998) account of "growing up digital" and the idea of the rise of a "Net Generation" and with the possibility advanced by Bill Green and Chris Bigum (1993) that teachers may be "aliens" in their own classrooms. It also provides a theoretical basis from which to approach diametrically opposed accounts of phenomena like "channel surfing," such as those provided by Henry Giroux (1995) and Douglas Rushkoff (1996) respectively.

Most importantly, however, the concept of mindsets provides a possible means for understanding and addressing the one-dimensional, inauthentic, "recycled school routines" character of so many classroom appropriations of new technologies.

A New Project

Within the context described in this chapter so far, a small-scale pilot project was proposed in 1998 to Language Australia, a national funding body for language and literacy research and professional development. The proposal was accepted and funded, and the project was implemented during 1999 (Bigum et al. 2001). The project aimed to test the feasibility of an alternative curricular and pedagogical approach to using new technologies in literacy education. It aimed to address three main concerns, as follows.

1. Teachers' cultural identities and experiences are often very different from those of their students. This makes it difficult for them to connect learning as closely as possible to students' varied cultural identities and experiences: that is, to teach for diversity and to minimize disadvantage. In addition to familiar issues of diversity and disadvantage associated with ethnicity, social class, and language, it must now be recognized that issues arise around how to relate teaching to the identities, experiences, and perspectives of increasing numbers of "screenagers" (Rushkoff 1995) and "insiders/natives" (Tunbridge 1995) who have grown up amidst the saturation of daily life by the digital-electronic apparatus (Ulmer 1987). It makes perfectly good sense to think of learners who are digitally competent being disadvantaged by learning arrangements that marginalize or penalize some of the very real proficiencies they have acquired.

2. Low levels of technical and cultural knowledge on the part of teachers often result in computer-mediated learning activities being ineffective, inefficacious, or mystifying. This may range from time being lost for want of knowing simply how to operate the machines to students acquiring odd or confused notions of a practice because of the way the practice is represented within classroom activity.

3. Teachers often make well-intentioned uses of student "savvy" with new technologies to get around snags at the technical operation level. If the practices within which these operations (and skill appropriations) are embedded are ineffectual or at odds with mature versions of computer-mediated social practices, the result of drawing on student savvy might be to enlist "insider/native" competence in the service of "newcomer/immigrant" practices.

The Logic of the Project

The idea behind the project was to build four purpose-designed networks of practice, two each in two cities 500 kilometers apart. Each network would be based on a school, although it was intended that network activities occur outside of formal school hours and formal curricular work. The networks would contain at least one resident teacher and two or more students from that school. In addition to the resident teacher (who would assist with accessing space and equipment), we planned to include a teacher currently in training. Each cluster would contain at least three students representing a mix in age, gender, computing experience, and personal cultural investments. In addition, each network would contain one or more "cultural workers": older youth or adults who were steeped in experience and who could represent insider expertise on aspects of social practice relevant to the activity of the network. At least one researcher and research assistant was to be assigned to each network of practice.

The project designers intended that each network of practice would work as a face-to-face group for two hours on a weekly basis over an eight-to-ten-week period, and that between meetings they would use electronic links to continue planning and implementing their activities. They also intended that the four networks be linked electronically to each other in order to exchange information, ideas, and experiences during the life of the project.

The aim of the intervention was to employ a logic of "scaffolded co-construction" in which participants, working collaboratively and in accordance with their respective strengths, could conceptualize and implement learning activities of an authentic and mature (or expert-like) nature. The focus would be on each network collaborating to develop some form of technological literacy that involved an electronic information and communication technology. We hoped that the intervention would foment a pedagogical logic that could work in mutually informing and potentiating (or enskilling) ways, with participants coming from varying mindsets, experiential backgrounds, and distributions of competence. We also hoped that this pedagogical logic would generally be adaptable to a wide range of educational settings.

The networks of practice were to function in accordance with specific operating and design principles. They were meant to recognize and engage the varying mindsets of participants, and, in particular, to identify and work with the available mix of "immigrant/newcomer" and "native/insider" sensibilities with respect to new technologies. The networks were designed to develop among newcomers and insiders alike an appreciation of the knowledge bases and mindsets of the other participants. Ideally, they would promote among all participants new technical skills with their selected ICTs, as well as cultural and critical understandings of literacy practices involving these technologies. Importantly, we hoped that research into the networks in operation would provide insights into how pedagogical and curricular approaches could be developed to promote such technological literacies effectively within planned learning contexts.

One of the planned outcomes of the study would be generic, proto-typical resources based on the research experience that could be modified for local use by educators. These resources were expected to emphasize the fostering of authentic and mature forms of practice, approximating insider views of how these things get done in "real life." Each network was to produce a tangible product in the form of a retrospectively constructed unit prototype that could serve as an exemplar of how pedagogy could proceed in school-based learning.

We envisaged an initial "warm-up" phase, involving activities designed to familiarize participants with the operating principles of the network. These activities might include playing computer games that involved seeing situations from inside a character's perspective. After engaging in these warm-up activities the networks would move onto the main agenda and negotiate what they were going to do and how they would do it, and then get on with doing it. Diverse kinds of activities were seen as possible options to be negotiated within the networks. These included:

- designing a web page for a client (such as an educator at a local university or a local industry group); participants would be involved in page design, construction, and publication.
- constructing a community database to be located in a particular school. The network would identify the kinds of information that were interesting, relevant, and important to the community, and then participate in the collection, organization, and on-line publication of this data.
- engaging in a geographic information systems mapping activity, possibly using university facilities—for example, mapping local skateboarding venues.
- establishing a youth-culture or emergent-artists' network, using online resources and facilities to inform the public about the network, to advertize events, and to facilitate activities.

Within each network participants would work together to decide exactly what they were going to do. This decision would take account of the means they had available to them within the network and via other resources (including expertise) they could access. The networks would be free to determine their own patterns of activity (if any) between sessions. It was important (and was factored as much as possible into the design of the intervention) that in conceiving, shaping, and implementing their activities each network would draw on their own skills and understanding. They would consciously pursue insider interpretations of problems and productions of outcomes. Since a range of mindsets would almost inevitably be represented in each of the networks. Identifying and negotiating across these in search of a mature or insider production would be a key element of the learning and doing process.

The researchers were to play multiple roles in this process. They would observe and document the activities in the manner of qualitative research fieldworkers. They would also, however, be available to offer expertise as required, and to monitor the extent to which authentic forms of practice—approximations to mature insider versions—were being pursued.

Upon completion of the projects, with their embedded forms of technologically mediated literacies, the researchers were to analyze the data, theorize what they had encountered, and advance interpretations, recommendations, suggestions for further research, and the like, in the usual manner of research reporting. In addition, however, they were to distill what they saw as the best educational qualities of the projects and assemble the cultural productions as prototypes for units of work to be undertaken in formal school programs. These prototypes would describe processes and products in ways that would map broadly onto formal requirements for curriculum planning in schools, such as orientation-enhancement-synthesis. The outcomes would combine structure and flexibility to provide guidance for others who wished to adopt a similar approach. It was intended that the prototypes would not be tight blueprints or "painting by numbers" formulae for classroom work.

This was the situation in terms of research intentions and aspirations prior to actually implementing the study. In the remainder of this chapter we will describe how things played out in practice in one of the four sites: Malveny State School. This site has been chosen for discussion because it provides a good example of trying to bring elements of wider cultural fields to the characteristic culture of schools and classrooms. It has also been chosen because the use of cultural workers and the availability of expertise in real-world social practices were particularly well developed at this site. In particular, the study at Malveny documents the work of an idiosyncratic cultural worker employed in the dual role of field-based researcher and cultural animateur.

A Note on the Researchers

The research sub-team involved with the Malveny network was comprised of two on-site fieldworkers and two full-time researchers working at a distance. The fieldworkers were responsible for locating the site, negotiating access, stimulating the project in the site, collecting data, undertaking preliminary organization of the data, and moving the data on to the full-time researchers for analysis, interpretation, and reporting. The researchers working at a distance received data from the fieldworkers in the form of video recordings of sessions, transcripts of interviews, brief written summaries of videotaped content, and written reflections and comments. They worked with this data in isolation from the study sites, but maintained close contact with the fieldworkers to clarify points, check aspects of the data, and receive feedback on draft reports.

One field-based researcher, Bob, held a doctorate from a leading U.S. research institution with a specialist program in sociolinguistic studies of education. Toward the end of the project he was appointed to an academic position in a U.S. university. The other field-based worker was Michael Doneman, who operates a consulting firm known as MWK (see MWK 2000a). Michael had extensive experience in conceiving, designing, and implementing community and school-based cultural projects. He had been purpose-picked for his dual researcher-participant role in the project for several reasons:

- His prior experience as a secondary school drama and English teacher
- His prior experience of implementing and supporting a range of innovative and successful cultural projects in community and school settings.
- His successful previous collaboration with members of the research team in the *Digital Rhetorics* project.
- His philosophy of cultural democracy, his praxis of social-cultural animation, and his track record of building good rapport and working relationships with members of formally designated disadvantaged social groups.
- His sophisticated technical and cultural understandings of new ICTs and of mature forms of social practice that employ these technologies.
- His familiarity and affinity with the insider/native mindset described above, and his access to volunteer cultural workers willing and able to participate effectively in projects of the kind envisaged. Michael was responsible for recruiting Miriam, an indigenous Aboriginal cultural worker in her 50s.

By social-cultural animation, Michael meant a form of cultural practice grounded in community arts and community development, which often involves elements of education, training and economic development (MWK 2000a). The work of the *animateur* is to help members of a community "find and fulfill active roles as participants in a cultural democracy." The social-cultural animateur's role is to "aid people to associate their individual development with the development of their communities, and to mobilize their energies for participation in furthering that development" (Goldbard and Adams 1978, cited ibid.). "The objective of building cultural democracy is to help members of a community to discover and express their own cultural identities and exercise control over their own cultural development" (Institute for Cultural Democracy 1998, cited ibid.). In the kind of social-cultural work undertaken by MWK an artist-organizer uses both arts and organizing skills to pursue the goal of cultural democracy.

In a characteristic example of MWK's school-related activity with a cultural-democratic edge, Michael had instigated a project with students from an inner-city school for Aboriginal ("Murri") and Torres Strait Island students. The school aimed to provide a pedagogical and curricular balance between Aboriginal and Torres-Strait-Islander funds of knowledge and culture and those of mainstream white Australia. Students spent half a day per week at a community arts and cultural youth space in Brisbane's inner-city Fortitude Valley called "Grunt." Michael had been a driving force behind Grunt's creation and its multimedia and networked computing dimension. The students spent their half-days exploring aspects of identity using conventional artistic means of painting, drawing, and collage. They also learned technical aspects of web page construction, including basic HTML and web page design principles, using digital cameras, manipulating digital images and anchoring them to web pages, and using flatbed scanners. Students gathered material for their web pages on walks through the Valley accompanied by teachers and volunteer cultural workers, using digital and disposable cameras, sketch books, and notepads.

The students began putting together their individual web pages by creating large-scale, annotated collages of aspects of the Valley that were significant to them. These collages consisted of photocopies of digital and film images they had taken of themselves, their friends and family members, and the Valley area, plus drawings and found objects (e.g., food labels, ticket stubs, bingo cards, and the like). The works were then pared back to key images and passages of text as each student prepared a flowchart depicting the layout and content of their web page. During the last month of the project these flowcharts were used to guide the design and construction of web pages (see, e.g., MWK 2000c).

The result was a series of compelling and evocative readings and writings of everyday cultural (re)productions of the Valley as seen through the eyes of these Murri and Torres Strait Islander children. The web pages presented photographic images of the participants in relation to the Valley's topography and aspects that served as icons or tropes for the multicultural life of the Valley. For example, one image showed a Murri student—identified as the photographer's cousin—sitting in the lap of a large statue of a

Chinese figure in the heart of Chinatown. Others captured distinctive Chinese architectural shapes in the form of pagodas and symbolic gates, or shop windows displaying the headless bodies of plucked ducks ready for cooking. These pictures graphically portrayed the enacted identity of these Aboriginal and Torres Strait Islander young people rubbing up against key elements of Asian ethnic identities.

Further images captured elements more directly involved in the students' own identities, such as photographs of Aboriginal mosaic designs set in the sidewalks. Others brought kinship together with vital aspects of popular youth culture and taste, such as the photograph of a Murri student drinking a McDonald's milkshake. The shake was purchased by an extended family member the student had met on his "field trip." Additional images of popular culture abounded, such as pictures showing students lined up at a McDonald's counter, and photographs taken while playing video games at Time Zone and Universal Fun City.

All of these photographs were accompanied by vivid texts that captured key moments in the experience of cultural and personal identity. One text, for example, related to an impromptu role-play that occurred in the street outside a shop. One student had mentioned how he hated going into shops because the shopkeepers "look at us as though we were going to steal something every time we walked into a shop." The teachers immediately orchestrated an Oprah Winfrey–type scenario, where one adult role-played Winfrey and the other adults and students variously played police, shop keepers, Murris, and audience. This episode was recorded in the text of one student's web page as follows:

> China Town lots of people
> Susan pretended to be Opal
> Winney and we was the audience
> One group was police the others
> Was murries and shop owners after all
> that we did some drawings (MWK 2000b)

Malveny State School

(a) The Context

Malveny is a large, relatively new and rapidly growing state school situated in an expanding middle- to upper-middle-class suburb in an Australian metropolitan center. The school's most recent annual report preceding the study identified 60 percent of school families as falling within the upper-middle class. It had 600 students in 1999.

The project network met for just two sessions, each of five working hours on two Saturdays, five weeks apart. The work site was the large, comfortable, and spacious school library that housed twelve nearly new Pentium II PCs. These were on a local area network (LAN) that connected all the computers to a "high end" server running Windows NT 4.0. Standard software applications were available, such as a word-processing package and a simple graphics/desktop-publishing package. Malveny did not have a scanner for student use, but it did own a digital camera. Since this was the responsibility of a teacher not involved in the project, the camera was unavailable for the project. The researchers provided a digital camera for use by the participants. The server included a CD-ROM stack, from which students could access information during regular school hours. The server and stack were located in a room separate from the main library housing the Pentiums, which was locked during the project sessions. The service provider for the school's internet connection was the state Education Department. Classrooms also had their own non–internet-linked computers.

Notwithstanding this wealth of digital technologies available within the school, student access to the computers and the internet was extremely limited and tightly regulated. Students could access only pre-selected (or what the school called "supervised") websites. "Web surfing" or using search engines was not allowed. Reference material for students' project work was held on the CD-ROMs in the server stack, to be accessed through the LAN. Although teacher access to the internet was less restricted, few if any teachers appeared to make significant use of the internet services at school. From information obtained about the school's computing culture it appeared that the emphasis was on passive browsing and severely circumscribed information gathering. The participating teacher in the project, Lachlan, did draw attention to the high degree of computer and internet access most of the students had outside school.

Local technological knowledge was very limited among the current school staff at the time. Indeed, it was described as being almost nonexistent. Control of the server, the library-based computers, and the network was vested entirely in a teacher's aide based in the library. The school librarian did not directly involve herself in computer maintenance or scheduling. She was actually quite antagonistic toward the computers—complaining that they were taking over her library and turning it into a computer lab.

Negotiating permission to undertake the project at the school and establishing the form it would take came down to meetings between Michael, acting as facilitator on behalf of the research team, and the school principal, Mr. Ruggs. It was clear that the principal favored a project that designed a website for the school. The participating teacher agreed that this would be a good focus, although prior to the first meeting Michael and the teacher (Lachlan) agreed to leave open the option of doing something else if the participants wished. As it turned out, the network agreed at the first session that building a school website would be a good thing to do.

In fact, the attitude of the school administration toward the project proved indifferent at best. They refused to allow the project team to pay Lachlan through the school accounts for his time. The "bottom-line" commitment of 20 hours in formal sessions was chopped back to 10 hours over two Saturdays as a condition of the school's involvement. Access to school hardware and software was restricted to the stand-alone capacities of the Pentiums. The key to the project proceeding at all from the side of the school was Lachlan's enthusiasm and energy.

(b) Participants in the Project Network at Malveny

Non-school Participants

There were three non-school participants in the project. Besides Michael and Bob (introduced earlier), the participants included Miriam, a highly respected Elder within the city's Murri community. She was enthusiastic about the project and about the possibilities technology might hold for increasing communication among people. As she said, "One thing about this technology that really I approve of is the availability of it to people to get in contact with other people, instead of the telephone. It just amazes me and I'm just wondering how much further it is going to go."

When asked how she perceived her role as a cultural worker in the project, Miriam answered, "From the perspective of an older person in amongst younger people creating web pages, and I don't know what sort of interaction is required [on my part], but I thought it was going to be fun in any case." She had agreed to participate at Michael's invitation with just a day's prior notice.

The School-Based Participants

The school-based participants consisted of Lachlan, three Grade 6 students aged about 11 to 12 years (two males and one female), and a male Grade 5 student. The students were all pre-selected by Lachlan (three were his pupils) and their parents were subsequently approached for permission. Lachlan's criterion for selecting these particular students was that he thought they especially would "get something out of the experience." All four were assessed as above average in most areas of their schoolwork, and all of them had had extensive experience with computers and the internet, mostly out of school.

The Teacher.   Lachlan was a Grade 6 teacher who was effectively the promoter of the project within the school. He was a competent word-processor and spreadsheet compiler, but during the network sessions, his role was that of a learner because many of the software applications (e.g., *Web Wizard, Paintshop Pro*) were new to him. Similarly, he had never before constructed a web page. Lachlan proved invaluable in smoothing potential problems of access to the computer equipment in the library. The librarian and other administration staff seemed to afford little trust to Michael and Bob and the project per se.

The Students.   Caleb was an articulate and poised Grade 6 student who thought that the project sounded "pretty cool so I might as well do it." He had never built a website before, but was quite familiar with computers and web-based applications. His family had a computer at home and every-one—his father, mother, and older sister—used it for various work and re-laxation purposes. Caleb told us he first used a computer before starting school. Out of school time, he e-mails his cousin and joins him in the Yahoo chat space on the internet (http://chat.yahoo.com). Caleb knows how to "ping" someone (as he puts it) in a MOO or chat space so that the message becomes private.

An interesting and revealing anomaly arose with respect to Caleb's computing knowledge, one that sheds light on his school-based and out-of-school experiences, and on his purposes and practices with computers. He explained how he went to use the internet for a project on Medieval times. He keyed in "www.medieval.com.au" for the URL. Not surprisingly, he received back the message "your URL could not be retrieved." At this point Caleb gave up, claiming that "it didn't work." Similarly, he was not au fait with different computer platforms and was unsure whether their home computer was a PC or an Apple.

Esther was also in Grade 6. She started using computers at a later age than Caleb and the other boys, but her computing knowledge at the time of the project was at least equal to, if not greater than, that of the boys in the network. Her family had internet access and a scanner at home, and Esther could use both confidently. When writing a text on plush toys prior to the time of the project, she had used the scanner to create an image of her favorite plush toy and imported it into her word-processed text. Es-ther had a good grasp of what a web page is, could use e-mail programs fluently to e-mail friends in Australia and relatives in England, and regu-larly exchanged website URLs with friends.

When quizzed about the sort of things one would expect to see on an official school website, Esther nominated "pictures of the school and of what kids do at school"—precisely the kinds of things that appear on such sites. At home, Esther's mother—a parent helper for the Grade 3 teacher— uses the computer to prepare worksheets. Esther's dad is a plumber who word-processes his quotes on the computer because, as Esther puts it, "he has really messy handwriting and he finds it really hard to read [what he's written], so he does it on the computer."

Bart was the third Grade 6 student in the group. He began using computers before starting school. "My first computer type was a Sega Master system, it was one of those little consoles of about six bits, so the graphics I think were about 2D." By Grade 1 he reports that he was playing *DOOM* on a friend's computer, and shortly after his family bought a home computer. By Grade 3 his main computer use was still gaming, especially "shoot-em-up games," "cause I love that kind of thing."

Bart soon began learning more about computers because "basically, I've played most of the games [on our computer] and just got maybe a little bored. I was just walking around my computer and basically just started learning about all the functions." He also explored "readme.txt." files and books about computers. He said he was a confident and capable user of Microsoft's word-processing package and *PowerPoint,* but that he used them only for school work. At the time of the project he had at home what he called a "game myth." It had an online multiplayer function built into it so that he could play the game with or against other people via the internet. "What happens on Multiplayer is you log-in and you can talk to people and actually play with the people and you can join up with teams and everything."

At ten years of age and in Grade 5, Charlie was the youngest student in the project. His family had an internet connection, and Charlie understood what web pages are and what they can be used for. When asked about school web pages he described many of them accurately, saying "They just have a basic web page for the start picture of the school." His father informed him that he began using computers when very young, around three years old. At the time of the project he did not remember yet having used the internet to get information for school projects, but thought he would soon "because I am doing a project on modern combat aircraft." One of Charlie's favorite websites at the time was one where "you grow this monster" and connect "them together [i.e., with other people's virtual monsters] and they have a battle." He learned how to construct and work his virtual monster by reading instructions on the web pages. Other internet-based interests include downloading card games such as 500 or baccarat. He was hoping that he would get a *LEGO Mindstorms* robot for Christmas.

(c) Prelude to Practice: Michael's "Metas"

Michael had developed a pre-planned flexible curriculum—a "tutorial"—
to use in sites like Malveny, as well as in community-based learning contexts. This tutorial drew on his diverse experiences over the previous 10 to
15 years. These included:

- experiences of designing and building websites in relation to his business activities
- pedagogical and curricular experiences as a former school teacher, his
  critique of conventional classroom learning environments and possibilities, and his evolving ideas of how to enhance pedagogy within
  "enclosed" learning settings
- previous work at the Grunt youth space where young people from all
  walks of life and with vastly different prior knowledges undertook
  "hands on" short courses to build their own websites for all manner
  of purposes—ranging from advertising their small businesses and skills
  to putting their upcoming weddings online.

The flexible curriculum based on the tutorial design proceeded in the sessions along the following lines:

- *Warm-up Activities* dealt with getting to know each other, checking
  out some websites.
- *Orientation* focused discussing functional and aesthetic characteristics
  of various websites, working out what was possible to do on the available machinery, within school protocols, and the like.
- *Web Page Construction I* was introduced by means of three categories:
  "graphics," "text," and "other stuff" (e.g., *.gif images, streamed and
  downloadable video, *Java* and *Javascript*, *Shockwave*, and *Flash* anima-
  tions, MP3 audio files, streamed audio, and so on). The function and
  use of Hypertext Markup Language (HTML) to bind media into a
  web page were also discussed by the group and demonstrated by
  Michael.
- *Web Page Construction II* dealt with creating hypertext/hyperlinks;
  planning the school website by means of drawing up flowcharts and
  organizing folders within the Windows directory structures (using
  Windows Explorer).
- *Graphics* focused on learning to move digital photos from the camera's floppy disk onto the computer network in the library, and how
  to store the images in files ready for "binding" into their various web
  pages.

- *Word Processing* was about using a word-processing application (e.g., Microsoft *Word*) to produce text for each web page. The group discussed the need for simple formats and fonts in web page design.
- *Interview and Reflection Techniques* focused on producing audio-recorded reflections on what students thought they had learned in each session. They were also introduced to the idea that they would interview each other at the end of the second and last session.
- *Project Planning.* Michael led a discussion on web page audience expectations and the consequences this has on the language and words used, the design and images. He discussed a range of constraints on web page building as well (web browser and website compatibility, fonts and general readability, colors and different web browsers, frames vs. no frames).

Figure 4.1 Introductory Lesson Plan

Orientation

- Introductory computer activity (game-based)
- Introduce/have students open Netscape 4.2 and log onto the network (may need short demonstration and guided appropriation)

Enhancing phase

- MWK tutorial (developed by MWK), which includes an introduction to HTML programming language
- Discussion of hypermedia and hypertext
- Whole group visit to 'GiantRobot' site
- Hands-on work categorizing (a) graphics (b) text and (c) other elements of web pages
- Introduction to paper/files and box/folder metaphors for developing a metalanguage for talking about organizing information on a computer; includes hands-on practice with storing, backing-up, and managing files (emphasis is on being tidy and methodical)

Independent exercise

- student establishes a personal file folder and complies a personal graphic folder using digital camera images, images downloaded from the internet, drawn in graphics applications, uploaded from a CD-ROM etc. and
- student builds a simple web page using an HTML application (e.g., WebWizard). Student saves work. Whole group discussion of processes just completed.

- *Content Collection and Development*. This was where the students began putting what they'd learned to use. They downloaded images and text from the web, took more digital photos, and managed their graphics files. The group also polished the development of a directory structure for storing the media they were collecting and for easy reference.

This curriculum process built on three key "meta" concepts associated with designing and building websites. The first was a three-phase tutorial plan developed by Michael, comprised of "Orientation," "Enhancing," and "Independent Exercise" phases. This is summarized in figure 4.1.

The second meta-concept was Michael's idea of websites comprising "Graphics," "Text," and "Other Stuff" all held together by HTML. This concept was made concrete and was constantly reinforced throughout the project by means of a tangible tool/device. A stack of diskette boxes was constructed as in the following figure. The device was kept in a prominent place and used throughout the learning process. Each box contained relevant color-coded materials used and produced during the sessions. (See figure 4.2.)

The third meta-concept involved flowcharting the process of building websites and web pages. In the learning process Michael used flow charts as a means for outlining and discussing the process and components of website design. The flowchart, as presented in the following figure, could be modified—enlarged, reduced, or simplified as needed—on the basis of group discussion about what could (not) and should (not) be included in the school's website. (See figure 4.3.)

Figure 4.2   Component Filing System

Figure 4.3   Example of Flowcharting the Web-Page Building Process

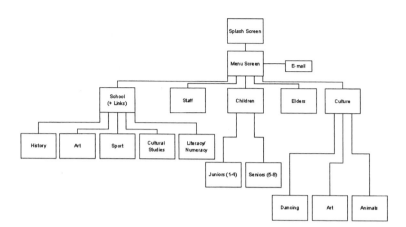

Over the two Saturdays the participants at Malveny spent a little less than nine hours in total of hands-on work: 45 percent of the "bottom-line commitment" originally envisaged in the project design. This, however, was as much as could be negotiated and implemented at this site. In crude time-and-motion terms, the tutorial was implemented over the two sessions as follows.

Day #1: Saturday May 8, 2000

9:15–10:30 A.M.

Participants engage in a range of "ice breaking" and "warm-up" activities. Initially, they get to know each other a little better by sharing information about their favorite food, favorite animal, the happiest moment in their lives, and the like. Warm-up activities oriented more specifically to designing and building a website begin with the students and the cultural worker pulling up the *GiantRobot* site on the internet and discussing its qualities as a site, its interest level for them, and so on. This is followed by participants exploring and discussing a range of school websites and other kinds of sites from the "Funnel Web" materials that Michael had purpose-assembled and loaded onto a CD-ROM for use in the project. Lachlan leads the students in discussing websites and pages in terms of an analogy to a book (turning the pages) and the possible purposes and reasons for building a school website.

> Lachlan: I'm interested to know what you think, all the different sorts of plans you could work for a website. Esther suggested that we go form a general one of the school and then do parts of the school. That's one way. What other ideas?
>
> Caleb: Start with the staff. . . .
>
> Lachlan: And go, where would you go next, what would your plan be?
>
> Caleb: Us.
>
> Lachlan: What other ways could you do it?
>
> Charlie: I think we should have a main page with a picture of the school, then we have like maybe projects, maybe down the bottom or . . .
>
> Lachlan: Here's something to think about. You know the one of going in further reminds me of an onion, and then you could have one that reminds you of goo, 'cause you're going, peeling off and going off and finding another thing inside . . . aren't you, as you go through them. . . . How about you think of a metaphor, something that hasn't got anything to do with computers, and how it can relate to a website? For example, the first thing that comes in to your head, give us something.
>
> Esther: Books.
>
> Lachlan: Books. Now how would that website be different? It would be like turning . . .
>
> Esther: Pages.
>
> Lachlan: Pages, wouldn't it? One bit would lead to the next bit, would lead to the next bit and so it would have a sequence. What other objects, give us an object Charlie.
>
> Charlie: Football.

Participants then explore and discuss "How Stuff Works." The students particularly find this interesting.

10:30–11:00 A.M.

The group moves from the computers to a round table area and Michael demonstrates some key underlying principles and concepts of web page construction using the conceptual model of "Graphics," "Text," and "Other Stuff" galvanized by HTML, and reinforced by the pedagogical prop described above. Following the short demonstration the participants move back to the computers to look at HTML as source code and in terms of how the *WebWizard* software handles the process of writing in HTML.

A one-hour break from 11:00 until midday follows this preliminary session, during which Bob interviews participants individually, while the others play games, discuss the project, and experiment with what they have newly learned.

12:00–1:00 P.M.

An intense one-hour session follows the interviewing. During this time participants are shown how to get into *Paintshop Pro* and access images taken earlier with a digital camera, and how to archive these in files and create folders of files using the file management function. With these fundamental concepts in place the group is introduced to the *WebWizard* software for making web pages. They spend 30 minutes exploring these concepts in practice on the machines, beginning by creating backgrounds for their "first attempt" web pages. The following student dialogue gives a flavor of the process.

> Miriam: This is the color that I'm looking at.
> Caleb: You want that color for your background?
> Miriam: I don't know how.
> Caleb: Click on that.
> Miriam: On this?
> Caleb: Yeah and move it wherever you want.
> Miriam: OK.
> Caleb: Now that's going to be that color for your background. Now you can move it wherever to make a different color and down there is all gray.
> Miriam: OK.
> Caleb: Go to "add custom colors."
> Miriam: Add custom colors?
> Caleb: Yeah. And then you've got to "OK."
> Miriam: All right.
> Caleb: Click on that "Select" and then that, that's it!

They move on to making dot point lists, inserting titles, and adding hyperlinks. The latter include links to files containing the digital images they had previously stored. By 1:00 P.M. the group has created some rudimentary web pages.

The group breaks for a pizza lunch between 1:00 and 2:00 P.M.

2:00–3:00 P.M.

The final hour of this first day begins with Lachlan and the students discussing the production of reflective journals on the project. Lachlan describes how journals can be kept and sets the students to entering (for ten minutes) some reflections on proceedings thus far. Suggestions for themes to make entries on between the sessions include looking for other school websites at home and recording their impressions and evaluations of these sites. Lachlan suggests they

> surf the net say twice a week, find one website that you like and write down all the different parts. What you like. Write down what the Website is, the website address so that we can go back to it ourselves and check on it and follow up your idea, that would be a good little bit of research to do. Pick two websites you like and then write down, notice what you like, details.

Michael explains how the journals can be useful in conceptualizing the web design in ways that are actually practiced by experienced web designers.

> You are going to be thinking about it on the way home from school or when you finish your TV program you will suddenly get an idea about how the website can be improved or how we would like it to go or you see a photograph in a photographic book or you would be walking along at the school at morning tea time and suddenly you will see a group of kids doing something and you will say "Ah, we should photograph that, that should be in our website."
>
> If I was planning a website I'd use [a journal], also if I didn't have the computer sitting on my lap and I had a pen in my hand I might start drawing a few things something like that, a photograph there and a photograph there and I wonder what we could do, pick up a text here and we went to here. . . .

Michael then raises the question of who the audience for the website will be.

> The school is saying we want a website, and you have to satisfy that client, so you need to carry in your mind, what is it that the client wants? So the school is not going to be very happy if you put obscene images on the website OK. But the other question is, who's looking at it, is it other kids, is it teachers, is it parents, other schools, the world, or all of the above. . . . That's very closely tied up with content and style, the next, you know again that's questions like, "Well we wouldn't have swearing on our website 'cause the client is not going to like it and probably the audience isn't going to like it." So that's a style *and* a content issue.
>
> What sorts of content? We've seen on other school sites, school photographs sometimes of kids and parents and teachers to give people an idea what the school looks like. Then we've got to go into planning and site design and . . . the next time we meet we'll go through the rest of this. I'll show you some more software too. . . . I've got a program that's much more powerful than [the *WebWizard* we have used so far]. It is harder to use but gives you a lot more flexibility. So you know how all our pages kind of look the same, different backgrounds and different pictures, but laid out the same.

This program will allow you to lay out all sorts of wild and wacky ways. So I'll teach you how to use that or I'll show it to you and you can learn how to use it.

Lachlan generates a brainstorming session and Michael records ideas on the white board as they emerge from discussion.

> Michael: But I think it's an excellent question, like if we are going to design a website for the school, who's it for? Is it for the students? Is it for the staff? Is it for your parents? Is it for the world at large? Is it for other students at other schools? Who might look at it much the same as you're looking at their work. Or all of the above.
> Charlie: I think it's mainly the parents and us.
> Michael: Not the teachers?
> Charlie: Um maybe. Actually the teachers could put down stuff like current events and stuff.
> Michael: Yes.

Day #2: Saturday June 12, 2000

The second session follows a five-week interlude. Apart from one break of 20 minutes there is continuous activity between 9:20 A.M. and 3:00 P.M.

9:20–9:35 A.M.

Michael begins the day with a brief demonstration of how to manipulate images in *Paintshop Pro,* building on the basic introduction to and practice with this software in the first session.

9:35–10:05 A.M.

The group spends 30 minutes discussing what they want to put on to the school website in the light of their thoughts and ideas since the initial session.

10:05 A.M.–2:00 P.M.

Participants are organized in two teams along a simple division of labor. Esther and Charlie work on the "Who we are" pages. Bart and Caleb work on the "What we do" pages. Miriam works mainly with Bart and Caleb. The two teams locate graphics of interest to be used on the pages, prepare text, and save their work to disk using the filing procedures learned in the previous session. From time to time they take a break to play a few games, but activity is mainly on task, as shown in this dialogue:

Michael: OK, so we have the page design as well. That's excellent. And Bart—

Bart: Charlie has got all our stuff.

Michael: Charlie has got your stuff.

Bart: Yep. We worked out what we were thinking of doing and we got to the attitudes, students, we got all of that so. . . .

Michael: When you say you got that, you mean you got text and all of that.

Bart: Yeah. . . .

Esther: We got together and . . . like here we are . . . and I did "What Makes Us Different." And I saved that on there and that's the writing and we filled out the home link button.

Caleb: And we thought we should put like a little . . .

Bart: House.

Caleb: No. A little pencil jar. Bart saved it.

Bart: Which I probably didn't.

Michael: Do you remember where it was?

Bart: Yeah, I could get it again. I also got some more things, that was like the triangle and the compass and whatever.

Esther: I got lots of Maths tools.

Bart: I know where I can get the pencil.

During the last 20 minutes of this long period the participants discuss whether they want to make a start on a second site that may be of greater personal interest to them than the school website—which had in effect been decided for them rather than by them at the outset. They decide against this, preferring to continue with the "official" school site and leaving the second site as a possible option for future work later in the year.

Between 2:00 and 2:20 P.M. they take a short lunch break.

2:20–3:00 P.M.

Lachlan works with the two teams to produce hard copy sheets that provide an overview of what they have produced. These sheets provide an overall sense of the layout and content of the various web pages created so far that will comprise the site. Lachlan consults with the teams about what text and graphics they have, what files they are stored in, and collates this information on the sheets. The sheets are given to Michael for him to turn into the finished pages and site later, because there has been insufficient time to do this during the two sessions allowed to them.

Outcomes

Although the time available in the formal sessions was less than half of what was planned for in the study design, participant indications of learning were numerous. For example, the students were asked at the end of the first Saturday session to write in their journals "what have I learned today and what do I want to know more about?" The students responded as follows:

> Bart: Today I learned how to make a basic web page, I had a lot of fun and I can't wait to learn more.
>
> Caleb: How to get digital pictures off the digital camera, how to play the X Ball, learning about graphic, text and other stuff and how to put a floppy in the school computer.
>
> Esther: There are steps here. We learned how to take photos with digital cameras, and we downloaded the photos onto the computer. And I got a picture of Charlie except I put it the wrong way around. We had morning tea and I learned to play about ten different games, then we learned how to create our own web page. Mine was great and was really fun to create.
>
> Charlie: On all our projects, since I have learnt to use the web I have also learned now how to use a floppy disk and how to get into files. I also know the basics of a web page.

Miriam's observations suggest that the students formed effective collaborative working partnerships and that within these Bart in particular made considerable progress in relation to the skills and understandings involved in building websites. There is also evidence that Bart and Caleb had no difficulty in identifying Miriam as a co-learner and work partner within what remained, essentially, a school setting. Miriam said:

> I did most of my work with Bart and Caleb, which I was really grateful for. And the interesting thing over the period of time, it was that Caleb took on Bart as his mate, more or less, to the exclusion of Esther and Charlie. And when we went out to do the digital [photos], because I had worked with them the previous time, Caleb asked "Can we stay in the same group? Can we stay in the same group, Miriam and Bart?" And it appeared to me that Bart was quite happy with that as well. But I just thought that that relationship between those two boys had grown considerably, to the point where Bart was starting to feel on equal ground with young Caleb as far as the computer.

Lachlan's perspective as the regular teacher of three of the students was especially interesting. He said that for the purposes of the project he wanted "some kids who are 'tech heads,' with that special interest [that] teachers perceive could get something out of this." He believed that they did, indeed, "get something out of it" although, with hindsight, a better gender mix might have been beneficial. In Lachlan's estimation,

As time went on, they each showed their strengths and weaknesses—they had potentials there. Esther I think, at her age, would have probably benefitted with another girl in the project. She had to sort out a lot in her head all the time with that, and at her age the gender stuff is a barrier she had to cross. Bart, I thought Bart grew articulately—his teachers were saying he's not that articulate in class. I think it was beautiful sitting on that seat near the end there and hearing just how articulate he was. And Caleb was a boy who's been, and everyone saw had a lot of potential, but has been irresponsible. I think his sense of responsibility shone in this project. He said, "Let's get in and finish it, we can do it." Charlie is younger too and we saw that the same sort of thing was revealed too, perhaps to a lesser extent.

In a limited but encouraging way, this chapter shows how even within a context where an "outsider-newcomer" mindset in Barlow's terms prevailed, there was still space to negotiate activity that was based on a very different culture of computing. The school leadership did not reject the project proposal, even if its original terms were somewhat compromised subsequently. In short, a conservative school leadership was willing to take a risk that it was not obliged to take. In doing so, it helped create a small window of opportunity for a group of students to access real-world expertise in a hands-on kind of way. This was a pedagogical setting in which work and play were integrated, where the mood was relaxed, but where the student participants were never off task for long, and where they admitted to learning a lot in a short space of time and to enjoying themselves in the process.

Even though this is an extremely limited example from which we are prepared to conclude very little, it is nonetheless an example that comes down on the side of running small risks, extending trust to learners that they will not abuse freedoms when they glimpse something interesting and worthwhile to be learned, and of opening up spaces for the play of an insider mindset within the context of classroom work. As such, this chapter represents a kind of research that is desperately needed in order to challenge the kind of constraining and obfuscating computing culture depicted in the following chapter and the assumptions and beliefs involved in sustaining it.

5

FACING THE DIGITAL CHALLENGE
FAR FROM TOWN

Introduction

THROUGHOUT THE 1990s, SUCCESSIVE AUSTRALIAN governments funded an extensive program of research projects focused on children's literacy. The program began as a key initiative within the Australian Language and Literacy Policy that was framed at the end of the 1980s and legislated in 1991. This policy was based on recognition of the fact that the contemporary transition from industrialism to post-industrialism, and concurrent changes in the role and organization of the state, greatly increased the stakes for literacy. Among the 16 projects funded to the end of 1998 was a two-year study of the interaction and relationship between literacy and technology in teaching and learning (Lankshear 1997; Lankshear, Snyder, and Green 2000). The research was undertaken by a consortium of investigators working in four of Australia's eight states and territories and became known as the "Digital Rhetorics project" (Lankshear et al. 1997).

The study was comprised of 11 "site" studies, involving 15 schools and 20 classrooms. The concept of "site" in this study referred to the location of activity (which was not necessarily limited to one physical setting), within which we focused on a particular participant or group of participants. This conception of "site" provided us with a fluid unit to study and analyze. One site, for example, was an electronic network linking several schools in remote parts of one state. Another site—the one to be described in this chapter—involved classrooms in three schools served by the same technology education adviser. Some sites were single classrooms, or multiple classrooms in a single school. Sites were fluid in the sense that the focus for a site was originally open-ended. For example, where the original site was a classroom, it sometimes became more telling to subsequently shift the focus to a teacher, a sequence of events, a group of students, or a set of practices developed around a policy or program, and so on. Hence, sites necessarily were not single well-defined units of analysis of the kind used in tightly designed qualitative case studies (Merriam 1997; Yin 1994).

Sites were purposefully selected to capture real-world diversity in teaching and learning practices involving literacy and technology. The site described in this chapter was identified by soliciting information from personnel in the relevant state Education Departments and from regional specialists. These key informants were asked about teachers, schools, and support staff in remote areas who were actively trying to find ways of integrating new technologies into classroom learning. It was not important how "innovative," "impressive," or "successful" the new technology practices were in the classrooms we were seeking. It was important, however, that the teachers and schools were not reluctant adopters of new technologies. The project was not aiming to coax educators into using new technologies. Rather, it was intended to provide an empirical base of extant everyday practices that were illuminating in ways—positive and negative—that could help contribute to enhancing uses of new technologies in classrooms by interpreting them in relation to ideas and criteria of good quality educational practice.

In short, the aim of the project was to produce a "patchwork quilt detailing the diverse models and circumstances that color current practice" (Lankshear et al. 1997, Vol. 1, p. 4). Sites were identified and investigated with a view to diversity and to providing "exemplars." Diversity was pursued by covering:

- a range of geographical locations—inner city suburbs, outer suburbs, satellite cities, regional towns, small remote rural towns
- primary and secondary schools at all levels from lower primary to upper secondary
- multiple "key learning areas"—English, technology, studies of society and the environment, science, maths, and the arts,
- sites in the three most populous states of Australia (New South Wales, Victoria, and Queensland).

By "exemplars" the investigators meant informative and illuminating examples of what is actually going on in everyday learning on an everyday basis, across a range of circumstances, policy contexts, resourcing arrangements, professional knowledge, and so on. That is, "exemplars" are examples we can learn from in constructive and productive ways. In this sense, the term "exemplars" does not imply "best practice," or exemplary in the sense of being ideal, optimal, or worthy of emulation—although in the overall study some of the exemplars came close to this meaning.

Working within a tight budget required finding strategies for covering as much ground as possible with as much methodological, conceptual, and theoretical rigor as possible, and maximizing the evenness of the study across all sites. Four main strategies were employed to these ends.

1. A site design matrix

The overall corpus of sites aimed to maximize coverage across four variables:

- state level (the three participating states)
- school level (primary/elementary and secondary)
- band level (lower, middle, and upper at both primary and secondary levels)
- urban and rural
- key learning areas

All but one of the eleven sites involved state (or public) schools.

2. An agreed range of types of data

Investigators each collected contextual or background data (e.g., about the school, community, local economy, and the like), relevant artifacts (e.g., policy documents, program outlines, lesson plans, samples of student work that involved digital technologies in some way), interview data, and observational data from classrooms.

3. An organizational template for site studies

Investigators used a template to frame accounts of the site studies. This template was developed at the outset of the project. Hence, although it was primarily an organizational structure for writing, it served to guide data collection, analysis, theme development, and interpretation. The template involved a uniform sequence of six components.

- *The study at a glance:* a brief abstract of the study including key points and issues arising.
- *The site:* a description of key features of the site, such as location, socio-economic profile, demographics

- *The policy context:* a description of main artifacts, including school policy documents, state and federal requirements, and relationships between observations and formal policy guidelines and aims
- *The practice:* key features of observed practice
- *Distinctive features:* elements arising from the site study seen as providing "exemplars" as defined above
- *Issues and implications:* issues arising for the investigators. These were informed by work done under previous headings, conversations with other investigators, feedback from participants in the "member check" process, and the like. Implications for pedagogy, curriculum planning, policy development, and future research were inferred from the issues and interpretations on which inferences were based.

4. "Snapshots"

Textual "snapshots" were used to capture as graphically as possible moments of practice in time and space within each site. These were what the investigators saw as significant momentary renderings and distinctive features of practice (ways of "doing" technology and literacy). The snapshots were composed and viewed against the background of the site and the policy context, and with a view to composing issues and implications (Knobel 1999; Lankshear 1997).

The Chosen Site: "Out West"

The site we discuss in this chapter consisted of three geographically remote schools in a large Australian state. Each school was located 700 to 800 kilometers from the state capital in the hinterland to the west. Two of the schools in this site were more than 300 kilometers apart. At the time of the study the state was divided into numerous education administrative regions. Each region had a head office and was served by a number of school support centers located in larger towns, and school support sub-centers in smaller towns.

Tipping, Manjerra, and Danton were schools located in the same remote school region and served by the same support sub-center. Despite the distances between them they shared three common features that galvanized them as a site. First, the same "education adviser" (EA) for the Technology subject area served all three schools. She was young, enthusiastic, energetic, and very proactive. Her role was to assist schools in using learning technologies. Second, all three schools belonged to the state education system. Hence, they all were subject to a common set of policy guidelines and parameters established by the state's English syllabus for Grades 1 to 10, its "Computers in Use" policy statements (DEQ 1995a; 1995b), and its funding allocations for computing. Third, all the schools were entitled to special Commonwealth funding from programs (e.g., Priority Country Area Program) designed to assist schools in communities considered to be isolated and/or of low socioeconomic status.

The three schools served ranching and farming areas. Wheat production was the main income earner, along with other grains, cattle, sheep, and cotton. The towns were all very small (up to 2,000 people per town). The nearest banks, government services, and shopping facilities were all at least an hour away from the schools in another larger, regional "hub" town. Tipping had a hotel, general store, and a railway siding, as well as its primary school. At the time the school had 53 students accommodated in three composite classes: preschool and grades 1–2, grades 3–4, and grades 5–7. There were 18 students in the grades 5–7 class, which participated in the study.

Manjerra had a service station, hotel, mechanic's garage, police station, and the primary school. The school had 46 students housed in two composite classes. There were 26 in a Preschool–4 class and 20 in a grades 5–7 class, with the latter participating in the study. Finally, Danton was a slightly larger town than the other two, located 90 kilometers from the nearest large town, and on a slow, narrow road that branched off the main highway. The town had a hotel, motel, service station, general store, stock agent, news agent, and several small businesses catering to tourist traffic to and from a nearby national park. The school was a combined primary and secondary P-10 campus, with 100 primary students in the Preschool–7 section and 20 in the secondary department of grades 8–10. The study participants from this school were students in the grades 9–10 business studies class, who were working on a project with the teacher during their lunch hour and other study breaks, and during business studies lessons.

Tipping's grades 5–7 class enjoyed a spacious, well-furnished classroom. On one side of the room desks faced the blackboard. At the rear of the room there were clusters of worktables, bookshelves, and a computer desk. The walls on both sides were lined with windows. The room led to an enclosed verandah containing more bookshelves and two computer desks with computers. On the opposite side of the room from the desks a doorway led to another enclosed verandah and a small room containing a computer, modem, and designated phone line that had been installed for use by students learning a foreign language via distance education services.

Manjerra's grades 5–7 class also was housed in a large room that was generously laid out. Groups of desks were arranged close to the blackboard, together with two computers. One had modem access and the other had a CD-ROM drive. A bank of eight computers lined the back wall of the classroom. An enclosed verandah that augmented classroom space contained long worktables used in art lessons.

At Danton, the compact classroom in the business studies center contained tables arranged in two horseshoe formations. The tables contained six electric typewriters, eight computers, and a printer. As in the case of the primary classrooms at Tipping and Manjerra, the walls were entirely covered with commercially and teacher-produced charts and posters pertaining to learning activities.

A Common Policy Context

Practices within the site were shaped by a common policy context with respect to computers in schools, resourcing, and language education (that is, English and "Languages other than English" or LOTE). At the time of the study the state Education Department had recently published two policy documents concerned with computing in schools: *Computers in Learning Policy* (DEQ 1995a) and *Guidelines for the Use of Computers in Learning* (DEQ 1995b). Manjerra had already developed its own computer policy, based on these Department statements. Danton and Tipping were in the process of updating and rewriting their existing computer policies.

The *Computers in Learning Policy* document (DEQ 1995a) defined "learning technology" and established departmental priorities. These were that (i) students will use computers to attain curriculum goals; (ii) students will develop skills and competencies in using computers and an understanding of the role of computers in society; and (iii) teachers will acquire skills and competencies in the use and application of computers.

The *Guidelines for Use of Computers in Learning* document (DEQ 1995b) defined the aims of computer use in classrooms in terms of enhancing achievement of educational goals across the P-12 curriculum within a flexible, responsive, and challenging learning environment. It established goals for students and teachers respectively. Student goals included developing skills for using computers for a range of purposes, developing "appropriate attitudes" about their use, understanding the role of computers in society, and being able to manage information and critically interpret and evaluate computer-mediated information. Teacher goals were to develop skills for using computers in administrative, preparation, and presentation work; to incorporate computers effectively into learning in ways that ensure equitable access, participation, and outcomes for students; and to participate in ongoing discussion and experimentation aimed at using computers in the curriculum. The *Guidelines* addressed a range of specific themes under headings like "Curriculum Applications," "Understanding Learners," and "Review and Evaluation." The section concerned with the English program mainly referred to using computers for word processing, but also mentioned critically evaluating "the image of computers in popular culture," the importance of understanding "the structure of [software] texts," and "the development of spoken language skills in the use of adventure and simulation software."

The resourcing policy situation was interesting and complex. In the early 1990s the state Education Department adopted an organized approach to allocating and purchasing computers through its Grade 6–7 Computer Policy. Schools were allocated computers for its Grade 7 students and, subsequently, for Grade 6 students. Allocations were tied proportionately to enrollments in these grades per school. No funding was allocated for computer and network maintenance, however. Apart from this formal government allocation, schools have also made their own purchasing decisions, which have often been influenced by parent associations who raise money for "extras" such as computers and software.

Hence, under the umbrella of a state-mandated Computers and Learning policy, considerable variation at the level of availability and quality of hardware and software is evident between schools. Similarly, decision-making about purchasing and maintenance at the school level varies widely. Rural schools especially have high rates of staff turnover and policies at the school level impact staff members who are appointed subsequently. Teachers who come later, and often for brief stays in these rural areas, often disagree with decisions and policies implemented by their predecessors.

The three schools had all used funding available to them under geographically and socioeconomically disadvantaged schools programs to build their technological infrastructure. Allocation of this funding, however, is often based on successful applications in accordance with government priorities. At the time of the study, Danton and Manjerra had recently been informed that their current submissions were unsuccessful because they did not meet priority criteria.

Resourcing was further complicated by isolation. The internet service provider (ISP) used at Tipping was unreliable and expensive, and the phone equipment and lines were old and inefficient. At all three schools, equipment repair was a nightmare. Servicing required sending equipment to the nearest major city, at least 700 kilometers distant. Technical advice was available from the nearest school support center, 500 kilometers away. Not surprisingly, teachers were wary of troubleshooting the equipment, and were loath to allow unsupervised use of equipment by students. At

Tipping, a hard disk crash had knocked out one of the two computers in the grades 5–7 classroom for most of an entire school term.

The language policy context was dominated by the state's *English Syllabus for Years 1–10* (DEQ 1994). When this syllabus (which was a significant departure from its predecessor) was introduced, the Education Department provided schools with formal guidelines to develop their school English programs as part of the syllabus implementation process. Advisers were appointed by the department to help schools throughout the state write their programs, which were then forwarded to regional offices for moderation. Thus, individual programs greatly resembled each other throughout the state, using identical section headings, similarly worded aims and objectives and, in many cases, lifting sections verbatim from syllabus documents.

At the level of program orientation, the syllabus referred to the nature and role of new technologies within contemporary everyday discourses and social practices, to which English teaching and learning must respond and be accountable. Despite such references, however, the syllabus in no way foregrounded or made explicit the degree to which new ICTs pervade daily routines. Rather, and notwithstanding its strong grounding in genre theory, the syllabus privileged literary and grammatical orientations that kept the focus firmly on conventional print and broadcast media (film, radio, and television) texts.

Prelude to Practice

Georgia, the learning technology education adviser, was responsible for promoting effective use of learning technologies in schools within a 300-kilometer radius of the school support sub-center where she was stationed. Not surprisingly, schools normally received infrequent visits, and urgent requests for assistance often could not be met for weeks. Her role included providing technical advice about hardware and software owned by schools, as well as lessons for teachers and students on using particular applications. She arranged exchanges and swapping of advice and equipment between schools. She also ran in-service training sessions for teachers at a regional center (approximately 100 km from Danton, 60 km from Manjerra, and 140 km from Tipping).

Georgia's energy, commitment, and eagerness to experiment underpinned the practices observed in the study. At the time, she was evaluating classroom use of an Apple QuickTake digital camera and a scanner within the context of activities involving production of presentations using the Apple computer software, *HyperCard*. Georgia carried the camera and scanner with her from school to school. Unfortunately for Tipping, Danton, and Manjerra, Georgia was being transferred back to classroom teaching in a different region the following year. All three teachers in the site study mentioned her imminent transfer and expressed concerns about how this might impact on their teaching and learning activities and personal professional development thereafter. They esteemed her professional dedication, after-hours work, and capacity for following through.

Two of the teachers in the study—Mary at Manjerra and Denise at Danton—had recently returned to teaching after having children. Mary was the principal at her school and had taken up the role enthusiastically. In a short time she had made considerable progress in substantially redirecting and rewriting the school's policies and procedures. She planned to enroll in a Graduate Diploma of Computer Education the following year.

Denise, who taught business studies, experienced the inroads made by new technologies especially strongly. When she began her career, schools used manual typewriters to teach typing skills, mainly to girls. When she returned to teaching, computers had replaced electric typewriters, the typing component of business studies had been replaced by keyboarding, and boys made up a large proportion of the class.

The third teacher, Teresa, had taught continuously at Tipping for ten years. She had majored in computing studies in her pre-service teacher education course, although she had found no opportunities to subsequently apply her studies (some LOGO projects and programming in BASIC) in class.

Students either lived in the towns or on outlying farm properties. Those living in outlying areas often traveled over an hour each way to and from school. Usually it was the students from outlying properties who were most familiar with computers. In part this was due to the growing practice of parents buying computers to assist with their businesses—keeping track of cattle-breeding programs, mapping rainfalls, keeping accounts and records. In other cases, families had bought computers for educational purposes and then adopted them for business applications as well. Many students had grown up without television because remote areas in the region did not have transmission access. During the previous year, however, introduction of pay TV by satellite had changed the situation for some. Nevertheless, in all three sites, students were often much more familiar with computers than with television.

Resources Used in the Participating Schools

The following list summarizes the resources used in each of the schools observed.

Equipment shared by schools and supplied by school support sub-center

- Apple QuickTake camera
- scanner

- Macintosh 630 CD computer
- cables connecting video recorder to computer

Resources used by Tipping

- Macintosh LC630—shared with the Grade 3–4 class
- Macintosh LC475, modem, phone line, microphones and Conferlink phone—provided by the Education Department for Languages Other Than English (LOTE) lessons
- external CD-ROM drive and HP Deskwriter 600 printer attached to above computer
- two Apple IIE computers and two Image Writer II printers
- a range of software including *HyperCard, Claris Works,* skill and drill games
- teacher- and commercially produced worksheets containing technical computing tips and instructions.

Resources used by Manjerra

- five Macintosh Classic computers purchased through a scheme run by a supermarket, in which shopping receipt values were rewarded with computers
- PC computer provided by the Education Dept. for professional development and housed in the library
- Macintosh LC630CD
- modem and phone line
- Deskwriter 600 printer
- dot matrix printers attached to Macintosh Classics
- television and VCR
- a range of software including *Claris Works, HyperCard, KidPix Studio,* CD-ROMs (encyclopedias, factual texts), internet connection and e-mail software
- print-based texts including encyclopedias and factual texts from school library
- teacher- and commercially produced worksheets containing technical computing tips and instructions.

Resources used by Danton

- four Macintosh Performa computers
- three Macintosh Classic computers

- Pentium computer, won by a student in an art competition
- Apple printer
- six Olympic brand electric typewriters
- a range of software including *HyperCard* and *Claris Works*
- teacher- and commercially produced wall charts containing technical computing tips and instructions.

On the Ground: Practices in the Site

(a) Technoliteracy at Tipping

During the term preceding the research, the grades 5–7 class at Tipping had produced a *HyperCard* presentation on Olympic athletes. Georgia had produced a CD-ROM version of the presentation and given it to each student in the class as a record of their work. In this activity the class had followed a chart outlining the generic structure (derived from the English syllabus) to be followed in constructing their biographies of the athletes. The outline included headings for Name, Date of Birth, Event, Background, and the like. Students had produced biographies using paper-and-pencil resources to write drafts, which were then used as the basis for compiling the text into *HyperCard* format.

At the time of the study the class was doing a unit on outer space using the internet. Materials relating to this activity included a wall chart of Orientating, Enhancing, and Synthesizing activities (phases used by teachers to plan a literacy unit of work) and a "genre structure" chart (both based on the English syllabus). Teresa had also located CD-ROM information/materials on Space to supplement what could be found on the internet and in print resources from the library. Teresa was keen for the class to use resources available on the internet, but because the networked computer was located in a tiny room away from the main classroom, working with internet-based resources could only be done with five or six students at a time.

Snapshot #1: Teresa

After school Teresa locates and bookmarks suitable internet sites on "Planets" to share with the students. The next morning she timetables the class to go to the networked computer in groups of six, beginning with the Grade 7 students. "The others will get a turn," she assures the rest of the class. The six students from Grade 7 go to the room with Teresa. Meanwhile, the remaining students independently continue their work in math.

Meanwhile, Teresa is finding she is unable to connect to the ISP. She repeats her attempts to log on a number of times, but without success. The Grade 7 students in the meantime have returned to class and continue with their math work.

Teresa recounted similar frustrations in relation to using the "electronic classroom" for LOTE lessons. Twice weekly the Grade 6 and 7 students participate in French lessons with students from four other remote schools and a French teacher based in a larger regional town. (Learning a LOTE is mandatory for Grades 6 and 7 in this Australian state, but since small schools cannot support specialist foreign language teachers, "electronic classrooms" had been established by the Education Department in schools like Tipping.) In an episode recounted from a few days earlier, the students were supposed to sit at the computer and download graphics provided by the teacher who was speaking to them using the Conferlink phone. The difference between audio and visual reception times resulted in the teacher's instructions failing to make sense to the students, and poor visual reception resulted in the students missing important parts of the lesson. To top it off, poor audio reception often impeded students hearing students participating in the other schools.

(b) HyperCarding the Environment at Manjerra

Mary, the teacher at Manjerra, had an explicit operating principle for working with Georgia at the interface of learning technology and curriculum. She explained that within the various computer-mediated projects Georgia's role was to teach the students "the technical skills." Mary's role was to develop and plan the activities within projects based on her knowledge of and approach to curriculum and pedagogy. Within the process of overseeing projects Mary would learn as much as she could herself in the way of technical skills, either directly from Georgia in the company of the students or, later, from the students.

In the project activity observed at Manjerra, the teacher had devised a unit of work on environmental themes to be produced ultimately as a *HyperCard* presentation. The focus for the unit of work taken directly from the English syllabus was "information gathering and the relevant use of technology." The project was a cross-curriculum activity including the key learning area of studies of society and environment. Mary had also integrated a keypals e-mail dimension into the larger project. Earlier in the year the class had engaged in an e-mail activity around the Transactional genre, focusing on "invitations and letter writing for different audiences." International e-mail contacts had been established at this time. E-mail was used as a medium for learning the text types in question. In the phase of a later unit observed by the researchers, the class, organized in small work groups, was exploring an environmental issue pertaining to the range of countries in which e-mail contacts had previously been established (Sweden, the United States, and Antarctica). Each group communicated with the contact person in the country they were studying. When they had obtained the information they wanted they would organize it in pencil-and-paper draft form, word-process it, and then assemble it as one or more "hypercards" as part of the overall *HyperCard* presentation the class was compiling. To make their presentation they were using the text type "information report" (as derived from the English syllabus).

Besides e-mail the students were using electronic texts on CD-ROMs—including encyclopedias (such as Microsoft's *Encarta*) and other reference texts (such as *Australian Endangered Species*)—to research their particular country and environmental issue. Library reference books were also available as part of the information base the students were using. The bank of Macintosh Classics was used almost continuously during the observation period for word processing work (for other activities as well as the *HyperCard* project) and math drill-and-skill exercises. Clipart programs were widely used to illustrate word-processed texts. While some students used available computers, the others were involved with an array of print-based texts in a range of activities: using library books and worksheets (spelling tests, comprehension exercises, and the like), writing draft copies of work in exercise books prior to keying them, and so on.

Classroom work at Manjerra (and Tipping) used a pedagogical approach that is very common in multi-age/level classes, and especially in small schools where a three-grade composite class might only contain 15 to 20 students. This involves the teacher in designing activities for individuals and small groups as the focus for self-directed learning. Groups are typically organized according to students' individual needs and abilities rather than by grade level. The teacher works as tutor, facilitator, or guide. Peer tutoring—which draws on students' knowledge and prior experience—is encouraged. Whole-class lessons are the exception to this general rule.

In terms of planning, a "unit of work" lasting from one to eight weeks is developed around a theme, topic, genre, or other organizer, and activities and lessons are designed in relation to this "integrating device" (DEQ 1994b, pp. 22–23). This kind of cross-curriculum work requires learning-outcome objectives (content, skills, attitudes, and processes) from the respective syllabi and for each year level in the class to be integrated into the unit of work.

At Manjerra the students moved freely and regularly between desk and print-based work to computers for word-processing, using clipart, CD-ROMs, or printing. This movement was not rostered or tightly controlled. It occurred smoothly, organically, and utterly without conflict or frustration. This pedagogical approach involves much "incidental teaching and learning," seemingly "on the run," to cater for different needs and "learning styles" (the teacher's terms) within the class. Where and when a particular student or group needs to learn something in order to proceed with their work, the teacher responds. In Mary's words: "multi-level classrooms are all about incidental teaching and learning and catering to the individual's needs." Typical examples observed at Manjerra included: Georgia showing a group how to capture a video image from a VCR and transfer it to computer; one student demonstrating to two peers how to copy and paste images from clipart into a word-processed document; Mary explaining to a small group of students how to complete a worksheet on reading comprehension; guiding three students using an overhead projector to enlarge images for tracing; and giving a student a five-minute reading instruction session.

Snapshot #2: Amy
Amy is 11 and in Grade 6. She is seen by the teacher as an "above average" student who is at ease with academic work. She works with apparent confidence in the classroom. We observe her helping another student transfer a document from a Macintosh to the IBM computer, import a graphic into this document from a clipart program, and then print the final text. During an interview with a researcher she checks her own draft using a spell checker. She tells the researcher, who notes her casual approach to the new technologies in the classroom, that she has been using computers since preschool, where they had been an integral part of classroom work.

The researcher asks Amy what literacy practices she engages in and what kinds of reading and writing she does in class. Amy responds: "silent reading, partner reading, spelling sentences in the morning, poetry." When the researcher asks about the keypals project the class is engaging in she appears unenthusiastic. In her view the advantages of e-mail over conventional post, like speed and reliability, are outweighed by what Amy sees as the negative quality of its impersonality. Indeed, she does not mention the names of her keypals. Instead she refers to them by country. "We haven't got a reply yet from Antarctica but we got one from Sweden, oh and from Florida." She uses e-mail "to write and ask for information." Amy informs the researcher that she corresponds regularly through written letters with a friend who is now attending boarding school. When asked if she would use e-mail to conduct this correspondence if it were available, she replies: "No, I ask questions on e-mail, but I write to Karen about what's happening."

Snapshot #3: On-the-run Interview with Student

Interviewer: Have you used books to help write this report?
Student: No.
Interviewer: Is there any information in books on this topic?
Student: Yes.
Interviewer: Why not use them then?
Student: There's enough information in *Encarta*.
Interviewer: Is the information better?
Student: It's more up to date.
Interviewer: What are the other advantages of using *Encarta?*
Student: You can print it out, you don't have to go looking for the book. Books are better if *Encarta* hasn't got the animal in it, you can look in books then.
Interviewer: What do you use e-mail for?
Student: We write backwards and forwards. We get information from them and they get it from us. Like how big Australia is and how big Sweden is.
Interviewer: What's the difference between doing that and going to an encyclopedia?
Student: If you get onto the internet it's got up-to-date information.

(c) Augmenting the Principal's End-of-year Speech at Danton

The "class" at Danton was not a single class at all but rather a group of students from the Grades 8–10 business studies cohort engaged in an extracurricular activity. This involved producing a *HyperCard* presentation to be used in the (rapidly approaching) end-of-year speech night. The presentation was designed to be integrated into, and to enhance the principal's speech by providing images of the school year. Some images were taken with the digital camera. Others were comprised of frames lifted from students' videos, as well as conventional photographs scanned into the computer.

The process of producing the *HyperCard* presentation had been broken down into tasks that had been allocated to individuals or pairs of students. The students had formally accepted responsibility for completing these tasks on tight and firm deadlines. This arrangement had been adopted because the end of the school year was only a week away, and Georgia would only be able to come to the school twice before speech night. Work on the project was done during business studies class time—other than when participants were taking end-of-year tests—as well as during breaks. At times the teacher, Denise, would meet with the team as a group. During these meetings, she would often exhort students to complete their tasks, remind them of the responsibilities they had accepted, and coordinate subsequent tasks in the light of what had been completed. In between students would report to her with photos, video segments, and other artifacts they had collected or prepared. A sense of urgency prevailed.

The context for this project was interesting. Denise said she believed it was very important for students from remote areas like Danton to have opportunities to experience the latest technologies. She remarked often about Danton's geographic and social isolation from "mainstream Australia" (her term), and expressed concern that important changes and opportunities occurring in the cities might be passing remote communities by—and, in particular, passing their young people by. She saw activities and processes involving digital cameras, scanners, multimedia authoring software, and the like as a way of providing Danton's senior students with the kinds of chances she thought urban young people enjoyed.

Hence, even though activities involving new technologies were slated for classes at Danton, Denise seized the opportunity related to the upcoming speech night. She saw that access to Georgia's expertise and the electronic equipment she could bring with her provided a pretext and a real-world purpose for organizing a group of students into an ad hoc project team to create a *HyperCard* presentation. Denise saw digital slide show presentations as the stuff of the contemporary mainstream—a commonly used application in executive discourse and business settings that was becoming increasingly popular within school activities. Consequently, Denise threw herself into organizing the project, securing and coordinating Georgia's involvement, and teaching and learning along with Georgia and the students. Her aim was to create an effective *HyperCard* presentation for a specific purpose within the larger life of the school.

During Georgia's visits, Denise and the students often joined together to learn specific skills from Georgia. Denise often hovered nearby when Georgia was working with students to complete a task like downloading images from the digital camera to the computer. She would ask questions and take part as much as possible in the lessons while keeping her attention on other things. Those things included overseeing students' test-taking and attending to regular classes in the business studies center. Meanwhile the project team worked on their presentation around the rhythms of regular class work being done by others. On occasion, however, due to the pressure on time, Georgia just worked as a technician to complete certain processes herself, rather than having and taking time to teach them to others. For example, on one occasion she spent a lunch break on her own scanning photographs into the computer.

Snapshot #4: Working Together

A lunchtime working session begins with an exhortation. "We're all in this together," Denise reminds the group, "otherwise it won't work." At first the students had been enthusiastic about the project, but as the end of term draws closer distractions have increased. These include accreditation tests for some students, as well as the sheer anticipation of the long summer vacation. The constraints around time and access to equipment are becoming urgent. The team has only two more days of access to the scanner, the high-end computer that Georgia brought to Danton especially for this project, and to Georgia herself.

Denise gives a summary of the previous meeting and prompts the students to recall the configuration of stacks she had suggested last time, which represents the "shape" of the presentation. It involves three stacks of unlimited "cards," or slides, to be developed around the outline the principal had planned for her speech. Denise suggests they should use just three different backgrounds for the presentation, with one for each stack. She gives a boy sitting near her the task of taking digital photos of the school garden and the administration block to use in the first stack.

Denise then talks about who the audience will be for the presentation—parents and visitors. She also emphasizes that in preparing the presentation they are actually working for the principal. The group catches up on where they are in relation to the tasks assigned previously. Some have been taking digital photographs of snack-shop staff and specialist teachers (music, physical education). Others have been interviewing staff and students, grabbing image stills from video and converting them to files, and creating titles or headings using text art software. For the rest of the session Denise checks progress on these tasks and works with the two students who have been given the job of setting up the cards on the computer. Because there is so little time she just shows and tells different students how to use the equipment they are operating, explaining as succinctly as possible what steps are needed to complete their respective tasks.

In the end, much of the fine-tuning, putting together of pieces, and final assembly of the presentation falls to Georgia and Denise. Enough of the assigned tasks have been completed, however, to ensure that the presentation is ready on time. The researchers subsequently learned that the presentation was a great success and members of the school community were very interested and impressed.

"Making do" Out West

It is difficult to resist the interpretation that the teachers and learners in the three schools involved in the Out West site were having to "make do" as best they could in their efforts to integrate new technologies into curriculum activity. By "making do" we mean using the resources and opportunities available to try to produce something that is serviceable. Perhaps the most dramatic instance was Denise's effort to cobble together a learning situation out of fragments of time and resources that were mobilized around an ad hoc opportunity presented by the end-of-year speech night. On the other hand, and to use a different example, there is something quite desperate about trying to harness narrow bandwidth and unreliable telephone networks to a foreign language pedagogy that relied heavily on downloading graphics as a stimulus to learning elements of French language and culture. In each case we find dedicated teachers working at and beyond the limits of their expertise—which in two of the three cases was strictly limited, through no fault of their own. Despite the limitations, they tried to make things happen in contexts where physical resources and technological support were in scarce supply.

Some interesting actual and potential cultural tensions emerge around these cases. We will address some of these tensions in the final chapter, in conjunction with tensions and paradoxes generated in other chapters. For present purposes however it is useful to consider how much of the diligent and dedicated activity apparent in these sites is in tension with the policy culture generated by the state Education Department and with the culture of mature computing practices in the world beyond the school.

For example, the state guidelines dealing with the use of computers in learning included such learning goals as "understanding the role of computers in society" and "being able to manage information and critically interpret and evaluate computer-mediated information." The snapshots presented in this chapter indicate serious strains here. To a large extent the uses to which the computers were being put in class were not mature or insider uses of the kinds we would expect to find among experienced practitioners using computers in real-world tasks. For example, when using the internet to obtain information, researchers do not consult "pen/key pals." They consult experts, or else they use a search function to locate information provided by people whose work they recognize as authoritative (on the basis of criteria or procedures they understand to be appropriate). Hence, with all the good will in the world, it is possible that teachers who are short on relevant experience may unwittingly contribute to students generating specific *mis*understandings of the role of computers in society.

The tension may run even deeper in the case of students learning to manage information and critically interpret and evaluate computer-mediated information. In the contexts we observed, the teachers were fully taxed in getting their heads around the "operational" dimensions of the technologies and/or in getting the technologies to actually work. By "operational" we mean knowing how to "drive" specific computer applications. It was difficult enough for the teachers to know how to ensure that the students learned how to use the computers to obtain information, or to ensure that the internet links were up to the task of accessing information sites. It seems excessive to expect that teachers will also develop teaching and learning activities concerned with understanding the practices involved at a cultural level and critically assessing or evaluating the information obtained. Yet this is what the policy guidelines enjoined. Indeed, the entire research project, in which the Out West site was just one among many, provided example after example of classroom activities involving new technologies being exhausted simply in dealing with the operational dimension of the practices involved, that is, learning how to perform the technical operations. This situation left no serious opportunities in which learners could address the cultural and critical dimensions of practice (Lankshear, Snyder, and Green 2000).

A very important dimension of tension is evident between the curriculum policy developers and teachers and learners in the classrooms around resource availability within a cultural context of competition for resources and performativity. From the standpoint of Education Department policy making, it was undoubtedly a good "cost effective" idea at the time to introduce computers into schools on a basis tagged to enrollments, but to leave maintenance costs to the schools themselves. Disadvantages were to be dealt with by means of project applications tied to government priorities. From the standpoint of schools trying to deal with the new and unknown, however, these arrangements created serious difficulties (especially for rural and isolated schools). They tended to lock teachers into spending scarce time and energy writing proposals that stand a good chance of being unsuccessful—as had happened in two of our schools. This time and energy could otherwise have been used by teachers to acquire greater operational, cultural, or critical competence with new technologies.

A further dimension of cultural tension around making do that is evident in these cases concerns the centralizing of resources and expertise that is structured into the role of the Education Adviser. New technologies are often at their best and can be used most effectively when they are integrated into networks of practice where expertise and resources are distributed, rather than where they are centralized and hierarchical. Hence, something as simple as the spontaneous use of a scanner or a digital camera to capture and disseminate things of significance at the appropriate time and in appropriate ways are hopelessly compromised and "complexified" in cases like Danton. Here again, students are at risk of mislearning the role and place of new technologies in contemporary social practices.

For reasons that will become clear in the two chapters that follow, we do not believe that this kind of cultural tension is simply a transitional state of affairs. It will not pass as schools acquire more infrastructure, nor even as teachers become more experienced in the operational, cultural, and critical dimensions of new technologies. Rather, it is reflective of an underlying and fundamental culture clash in computerized classrooms.

"Making do," coping with new technical demands, and the resulting tensions that emerge, are just some of the things that occur when a new social technology is imposed on an existing social technology—particularly when, as in the current conjuncture, this is part of a much larger process of cultural change caught up in a new form of globalization. We will return to the theme of cultural tension and paradox in the final chapter, and in light of further cases to be reported in the next chapter.

6

GRID.FOR.LEARNING
@CLAMPDOWN.EDU

Introduction to the National Grid for Learning

BRITAIN'S NATIONAL GRID FOR LEARNING (hereafter, "the Grid") began as a government policy initiative in 1996 and "opened for business" in late 1999. Officially described as "a Government initiative to help learners and educators in the U.K. to benefit from information and communications technology" (BECTA 2001a, p. 1), the Grid is a "vital part of The Government's commitment to the creation of a connected learning society in which learning is increasingly accessible and adapted to individual needs" (ibid.). According to Prime Minister Tony Blair (1999),

> Not only will digital technologies become a normal part of everyday life, but Britain's international competitiveness will increasingly depend on the way in which we adopt them. Used well, they have the potential to improve achievement in our schools and colleges, to boost the prospects of British industry and commerce, to offer opportunities to all learners and particularly to those who would otherwise be excluded, and significantly to enhance our quality of life. In parallel, the Government is investing very substantial new resources in a programme to raise standards in schools and increase opportunities in lifelong learning. The National Grid for Learning will play a crucial part in this process. (p. 1)

The Grid's stated purpose is to help raise education standards by providing teachers, students, and education institutions with access to information and communications technologies (ICTs). Specific objectives for the Grid include achieving a new digital technology access baseline for educational achievement in relation to ICT, and addressing five challenges identified by the government in 1998 in consultation with parents, educators, and industry. These challenges (target year 2002) involve:

- connecting all schools, colleges, universities, and libraries and as many community centers as possible to the Grid
- ensuring that serving teachers feel confident and are competent to teach using ICT within the curriculum; and that librarians are similarly trained
- enabling school leavers to have a good understanding of ICT, with measures in place for assessing their competence in it
- ensuring that general administrative communications between education bodies and the government and its agencies cease to be largely paper-based
- making Britain a center for excellence in the development of networked software content, and a world leader in the export of learning services (BECTA 2001b, p. 1)

Main target users include teachers and students from primary schools, secondary schools and higher education, industry people, communities, and people involved in life-long learning.

The Grid as Infrastructure, Content, and Practice

The Grid consists of computer hardware, software and peripherals, internet connections and local area networking hardware and software. By mid-2001 the government had invested more than £650 million supporting Grid development up to 2002, and had pledged a further £710 million for 2003–2004 (Heller et al. 2001, p. 1). Expenditure covers physically equipping schools, colleges, libraries, and community centers with computers and internet connections, providing internet-based content, and enabling teachers and lecturers to access professional development resources. By late 2001, computers in U.K. schools totaled almost 1.1 million at an average of 34 desktop computers per school—although 25 percent of these computers are identified as being "ineffective for curriculum use" (BESA 2001, p. 1). According to published estimates, by late 2001 almost all schools in the United Kingdom had internet access, with an average of 75 percent of computers in each school linked to the internet. In these schools almost half the students used the internet daily (ibid.).

The government envisages highly interactive, global, and well-informed learning activities for in-class use. It intends the Grid to include indices and links to "worldwide sources and data" to support homework, information services (that is, parental access to general school information), and chat space for teachers to share teaching ideas and experiences (Blair 1997). In a position paper, the U.K. government urged industry to produce "high quality learning software, broadcast programming and online content," seen as "essential to the success of the [Grid] initiative" (DfEE 1999, p. 1). The government simultaneously pledged funds to schools for "content purchase" and for schools and learners to develop content themselves. A "New Opportunities Fund" provided £50 million to digitize content in libraries and other public institutions like museums and galleries (ibid., p. 15).

By late 1999, the Grid contained over 250,000 documents from over 250 different sites, ranging from content offered by software developers and textbook publishers to resources produced by individual teachers and pupils (BECTA 1999, p. 1, 6). Despite the government allocating 15 percent of the total Grid budget for "digitizing educational content" (Peters 2000, p. 26), content access and development has come under fire from several quarters. The software industry "complains that too much is being spent on hardware, and more schools are paying out of their own pockets for online software" (ibid.). Numerous educators believe the Grid initiative should invest in software development to be made available to schools free of charge, instead of schools duplicating localized software purchases (ibid.). Others believe too much has been invested in infrastructure and not enough in content development. Little specific information regarding content exists, and content development appears ad hoc at present.

The British Educational Communications and Technology Agency (BECTA) is in charge of designing and developing the National Grid for Learning "portal"—the main website for the Grid (NGfL 2001a). BECTA is also responsible for monitoring Grid use and safety, and for coordinating diverse input and services from public and private bodies, organizations and individuals (such as regional community groups; national charities such as Help the Aged; agencies and bodies such as the Teacher Training Agency; and others such as Hodder Science and Espresso Productions). With respect to "what people do with the infrastructure and content" (BECTA 1999, p. 6), by early 2002 no readily accessible information was available on the effectiveness of using the Grid in school contexts.

The Grid Today

The Front Page

As this book was going to press the front page of the Grid portal had just been changed—indicating one of the hazards of researching such a dynamic phenomenon as the WWW. The changes involved a new organizational logic, with different categories of content and pathways for accessing content. We have accommodated the changes to the fullest extent possible under the constraints of publishing schedules. This is a well-known hazard of researching the internet. Researchers and readers need to accommodate quick and unanticipated changes and to recognize the extent to which changes are culturally significant, at one extreme, and more or less surface level changes at the other. If anything, the changes made in 2002 actually strengthened the line of critique of Grid culture that we advance in this chapter. Certainly, the GridClub material on which much of our argument rests remains typical of the kind of fare available for younger users of the site.

The original portal featured a button bar running across the top of the page, with buttons for accessing different categories of content such as: "What's New," "e_Commerce," "Media," "Jobs," "Grid Safety," and "Link Your Site." The "What's New" button was typical in that it presented a categorized list of hyperlinks that led to sites new to the Grid or that were being showcased that month. The 2002 changes replaced the original large categories, and the portal was rearranged according to three specific, cross-referenced, user-targeted categories: "WHAT are you looking for?," "WHERE are you?" and "WHO are you?" Within these headings, much of the content remained the same and similar to the original.

The changes to the portal in 2002 were informative in their own right, and confirmed for us that the site was under ongoing review and revision. For example, in the original Grid portal website the *@school* website, which is a subscriber-pays site of school subject exercises, headed the list in the e-commerce category. In the rearranged version, it tops the list of hyperlinks under the "Learning Resources," "Games and Quizzes," and "Subscription services" sub-categories of the "What are you looking for?" meta-category. It is also found under the sub-category "Children" in the "Who are you?" section of the new Grid portal.

Subscription fees to *@school* are stepped: For schools with 75 or fewer pupils it costs £88.12 annually, 76 to 150 pupils cost £176.25, and 150 or more pupils cost £235. For parents and "home users" a subscription costs £35.99 annually. The *@school* site received a British ICT industry award, the BETT award, in 2001. According to the website, "every @school activity can be printed and used as a worksheet" (Pedagog 2001 tour).

In the current version of the Grid portal, the "What" category presents a menu of hyperlinks, organized into sub-categories including "Learning resources," "Games & quizzes," "Lesson plans & worksheets," and the like. Similarly, the "Who" link on the front page of the Grid portal takes the user to a menu of sub-categories such as "Children," "Parents," "Teachers," and "Students." (NGfL 2002a, p. 1). The "Children" sub-category is comprised of a list of websites ranked according to target age ranges. It includes online tutorials and quizzes in all school subject areas, online museums (e.g., information pertaining to Ancient Egypt, art and archeology online museums), information sites (e.g., data pertaining to the U.K. government), the BBC education pages, and the like.

The "Where" button takes the user to a clickable map of the United Kingdom. It also includes a menu of hyperlinks relevant to users in Scotland, Wales, and Ireland, as well as to the nine regions of England. The map or menu can be used to "find resources that are relevant to your region, such as community grids for learning, local projects, museums or libraries" (NGfL 2002b, p. 1). Each member country and region of England is responsible for developing a section of the National Grid for Learning specific to its cultures, populations, contexts, and school systems (but in keeping with the rules, regulations, and visions set down by the U.K. government). Community groups and schools may contribute content to the Grid, along with commercial content providers who span regions and countries. Each of these 12 geographical categories is sub-divided into menus of links pertaining to national sites, community grids, libraries and archives, and museums and galleries. Originally, each of these sub-categories was a major category listed on the front page of the Grid portal and, apart from the "community grids," these sub-categories are relatively self-explanatory. Community grids have been developed by communities within the United Kingdom to provide material for a range of people from youth—from around 10 years to 25 years in age—through to adult education students and on to senior citizens

The front page of the Grid website is divided into three distinct columns. The first column contains two sets of menus. The first set contains the three main organizing devices (What?, Where?, and Who?), while the second set focuses on information that supports the Grid itself. Included in the second column is a link to a News section that focuses on education-related items (for instance, a story on fathers being encouraged to become more involved in their sons' education). Other sections include a "What's new" link that showcases websites that have been recently added to the Grid network; a "Features" link, which focuses on current events in the academic year (such as exams and exam revision) as well as different teachers' or schools' favorite websites; a link to background information on the Grid itself; a network search engine service; and a link to guidelines as to what counts as safe and proper practice within the Grid.

The center column is devoted to content listing, which generally consists of hyperlinks to websites that form part of the overall Grid network (which extends far beyond the actual portal website). These content lists vary according to which category and sub-category the user is accessing.

The right-hand column generally provides related links to content in the "What's new" and "News" sections of the Grid portal. For example, at the time of writing and within the "Children" sub-category of "Who are you?," the right-hand column lists links to: the meningitis information website, a new and official Roald Dahl website, and a news item about students performing mystery plays in a cathedral.

Scope of the Grid

Before turning to more specific considerations of form and content of the Grid, which is our focus here, it is helpful to get a sense of its size and scope. As we have already mentioned, the portal website covers all four countries within the United Kingdom. Within Wales, Scotland, and Northern Ireland, and within each region of England, local governments and schools may contribute content to the Grid, along with commercial content providers who span regions and countries.

The Grid is concerned not only with classroom-based learning. The community grids, for example, are intended to support learning activities that are not necessarily tied to classrooms and, indeed, to a large extent will not be. A brief look at typical examples of community grids is useful for conveying a larger sense of what the Grid is like than is possible by considering the Grid in relation to school-based learning alone.

Community Grids

The community grids are accessed via the "Community Support" sub-category, by way of the large "Who are you?" category on the front page. By early 2002 there were approximately 25 Grids developed by communities throughout the United Kingdom. These community grids have been established by local groups, partnerships or communities that share a common interest. For example, the Yorkshire and Humberside region of England lists four Community grids: Bradford, Sheffield, Shipley, and Wakefield. The Bradford Community Grid (Bradford Council 2001) is a cornucopia of hyperlinks. Predominant categories include Business, Education, Local Links, Art & Culture, Entertainment, and the like.

The Business web page provides an overview of local businesses and the council's business strategy for the area. The Art & Culture web page has links to information about local museums, play houses, and festivals. The

Education page provides a local education news service, an overview of education in Bradford, an information page about outdoor education centers in the area, and links to education-related resources. The "For Young People" section of the Bradford Community Grid includes a link to an information page about the Bradford Central Library's Homework Center, and information for young people under 25 about career options, health and relationships, travel and study abroad, and so forth. Further information accessible from the Bradford Community Grid includes town council contact and activity information, links to online council services (such as paying taxes online, bill paying services, etc.), a report on local race relations, and the like.

Other Community Grids within the Yorkshire and Humberside region have different specific emphases, but basically serve the same purpose of co-ordinating and cataloguing learning projects and community services within the region. For example, Shipley's Community Grid, titled *Shipley Communities Online* (Shipley Council 2001), emphasizes adult learning and work—with special links to information about child-care services and training opportunities. Sheffield's Community Grid, *Citinet* (Sheffield Council 2001), is a network of adult learning courses and services, rather than an information and service site. Wakefield's Community Grid is titled, *Go WILD: Wakefield Internet Learning Domain* (Wakefield Council 2001). It provides news about local schools and teaching, access to education reports, linking to teacher resources for a range of curriculum areas, and showcases student work.

This sampling is typical of the Community Grids and illustrates how communities have opportunities to set up their own sections of the National Grid in ways felt to best suit perceived needs of local communities.

The Grid and School-based Learning

Through the Grid, users can access diverse topics pertaining specifically to primary and secondary levels of education in the United Kingdom (NGfL 2002c). Examples of topic areas include "Building the Grid," "Computers for Teachers," "GridClub," "National Curriculum," "Parents' Centre," "The Standards Site," "TeacherNet," and "Virtual Teacher Centers" for teachers in Scotland, Wales, and England. "Building the Grid" provides information for schools and teachers on contributing content to the Grid and using the Grid effectively in schools. "Standards" is also aimed directly at teachers and schools. Its chief role is to offer guidance to and suggestions for raising students' achievement standards. "TeacherNet" provides educators with access to government information concerning education as well as to services and resources for teachers (with over 1,000 lesson plans available).

These pages are reached via links from the "Teachers" subcategory under "Who are you?" The "Parents' Centre" is hosted by the Department for Education and Skills and provides parents and caregivers with information, advice, and guidelines for how they can best help with their children's education. It is reached by way of the "Parents" subcategory under "Who are you?" The "National Curriculum" website links every section within Key Stages 1 to 4 of the National Curriculum to online resources for teachers.

For present purposes we will focus on the GridClub and on the Grid Safety page(s). These give particularly revealing insights into what the National Grid for Learning means for school education in terms of appropriating virtual space for Britain's school education effort.

GridClub

A striking feature of the resources pertaining to school-based learning is the relatively small proportion of dedicated pages and topics addressed to the learners themselves, although this seems to be increasing slowly. Topics overwhelmingly pertain to teachers, governors/managers, and parents. One of the very few websites dedicated to learners, and in this particular case to younger learners aged 7 to 11, is GridClub (NfGL 2001a). This is introduced as being fun, safe, and "designed for kids to use at *HOME* or school" (ibid., p. 1, emphasis in original). The GridClub can be accessed via multiple paths from the Grid portal, or it can be accessed directly via its URL (http://www.gridclub.com). A key feature of the recent organizational changes to the Grid portal is that many, if not most, pages are cross-referenced to multiple categories, and not reached via a single directory path any more.

According to promotion on the website, every effort has been made by GridClub creators to engage children between the ages of 7 and 11 using cartoons and on-line games as well as by encouraging their own hobbies and special interests outside of school. All GridClub's interactive games, ideas, and activities have been designed by teachers and cover the National Curriculum at Key Stage 2. Adult mediators in the GridClub clubs interact with children and support them within the actual online discussions organized according to interests and hobbies (GridClub 2001a, p. 1).

There are three key areas or services within the GridClub website. "Have a Go" is open to anyone, as is the "Look it Up" reference section. The third area, the clubs themselves, are open only to children aged 7 to 11 and can only be joined via one's school. "Have a Go" contains literally hundreds of activities and exercises related to National Curriculum subjects (e.g., pertaining to scientific principles of angle and force). "Look it Up" is a reference section that includes an online dictionary, thesaurus, and a "clickable" atlas. "Homework High" is a relatively recent addition to this reference section of GridClub, and is organized according to secondary school subject areas. It is sponsored by Learn.co.uk, a commercial online index to teaching resources. Each area allows students to post a homework related question, to be responded to by "resident experts."

Questions posted by users within the section on English include:

• I have a 700–1000 word essay to write about "Great Expectations." I need to know what to write about for the question "What changes do you see Pip go through up to chapter 19?" I need to write about various different types of change and give references to them in the book. I have been told that chapter 19 in particular is a significant chapter concerning change. Thank you for your help.
• Is Philip Larkin essentially pessimistic? Help Please!!!!!!!!
• What is a proscenium arch stage?
• Hi I have to write a story on Harry Potter. Can you help?
• I have got my year 10 English exam on friday and was wondering if you could give me any info on this poem and short story: "Telephone Conversation" by Wole Soyinka.

The questions and answers are archived and searchable. Each subject section also includes a chat service.

Restricted access to the clubs section of the GridClub website makes it difficult to describe the clubs in detail. The clubs include: Outdoor Adventure, Animals, On The Move, Collectors, Sports, Football, and the like. Some clubs, such as the Outdoor Adventure Club, appear to be for chatting about activities and interests. Others, such as the Animals Club, provide members with information on a range of topics relevant to the club, include games on their website, and give members opportunities to interact online about their shared specific interests in what are labeled "miniclubs" (e.g., saddle club, dinosaur club). Each club is overseen by "grown up club leaders" (GridClub 2001c, p. 1).

GridClub's ostensive purpose is to provide young students with online spaces to pursue their own interests. Much of the site, however, is given over to "learning activities" constructed in an exceedingly school-like way. The "Tell Tales" (or "subject English") category within the "Have a go" section of the website is a case in point. The "Owl stories"—promoted as "four great stories to keep you amused" (GridClub 2001d) and connected with the Literacy Hour initiative—are really drill-and-skill activities in narrative guise. The first of the two Owl stories, *Ozzie Takes a Ride* (Oz New Media 2001a), aims at Grade 3 students. The text itself is reminiscent of slide shows, with one fixed backdrop following on from the other in a linear, sequential manner. Although some of the images involve simple animation, the interface looks and feels like a teacher-made resource, rather than a slick, seamless, attention-grabbing production such as those found in Dorling Kindersley or Bröderbund CD-ROMs.

Ozzie Takes a Ride also takes every opportunity to create "teachable moments"; such as when Ozzie the cat and Archie the dog are playing badminton. As the shuttlecock is hit between the two players, it first sails over the clothesline "net" with a big smile on its face, saying "happy." The next screen shows the same shuttlecock flying back over the net with a frown and saying "unhappy." The very next screen reads: "Did you see what happened when *un-* was added to *happy?* The word *unhappy* was created, which is the opposite, or antonym of, *happy"* (ibid., original emphases). This is repeated for the "dis-" prefix. At this point, the "story" becomes an exercise in making the antonyms of a given set of words by clicking on the appropriate "un-" or "dis-" prefix. It then moves onto a classifying activity, followed by an exercise requiring the student to distinguish between examples of rhymes and cinquains. A exercise on using the table of contents in a book to "zero in on" needed information comes next. This is followed by a brief history of bone collecting, and so on. The narrative glue holding the drills together is, at best, thin.

Safety and Propriety in the Grid

BECTA has been assigned the task of establishing clear guidelines as to what counts as safe and proper practice within the Grid. Two main roles are involved. One is to define, monitor, and, so far as possible, exercise control over acceptable content generated by schools, local councils, commercial ventures, and the like, within Grid-linked sites. The second role involves providing guides to the appropriate use of Grid content. This partly consists of explaining intellectual property rights and guides to "fair use" of content found on the Grid (many Grid-linked sites have been built and are maintained by commercial companies averse to plagiarism). But the concern with propriety has been extended beyond minimal guidelines, imposing conceptions of appropriate practice in a wider and more invasive sense, as we will discuss below.

To pursue these ends, BECTA has produced an information website known as "Superhighway Safety" (DfES 2001). Britain's Minister for Early Years and School Standards, Catherine Ashton, outlines the mission to be served by the site as follows:

This Government wants everyone to have access to the wealth of cultural, scientific and intellectual material to be found on the Internet. But we are equally determined to ensure that students are protected from unsuitable material and that we all use the equipment we have properly. We all share a responsibility to make sure that students' use of the Internet is appropriate and safe. (Ashton 2002, p. 1)

With respect to protecting learners from "unsuitable material" on the internet, the government has undertaken several initiatives. One is Gridwatch, which incorporates "a vision for the roles and responsibilities of teachers, parents and students" when using the Grid (Ashton 2002, p. 1; DfES 2001, p. 8). Gridwatch is a service for reporting unsuitable material encountered on the Grid, as well as for users to offer feedback on the quality, currency, and accuracy of information available on Grid-linked sites. Gridwatch promotes other safety measures as well, including the following:

- "Walled gardens." This is a paid subscription service that "offers subscribers access to collections of pre-selected Web sites. Walled Gardens offer the highest form of control and protection against users intentionally or inadvertently accessing inappropriate material" (DfES 2001, p. 3).
- Filtering and site-blocking software. These software programs search for potentially unsavory words in web page and e-mail texts and block access to e-mail or websites where it is found.
- Usage tracking software. This enables teachers to "track" the websites students have visited or tried to visit.
- Firewalls. These are programs that sit on a network and block or control entry to and exit from areas it is protecting.
- "User contracts with children" (Ashton 2002, p. 1) and signed "codes of conduct" for all learners. Users under 18 years of age need to have their signed codes countersigned by caregivers (DfES 2001, p. 1).
- Impressing on students the importance of never giving out their personal details (name, age, address, etc.) in their e-mails or online chat.

The "Superhighway Safety" site also lists diverse non-Grid websites dealing with the safety of children on the internet for teachers and parents to read, and presents examples of what its creators regard as excellent practice. Denbigh School offers a typical case.

Denbigh School, a technology college for 12- to 18-year-olds in Milton Keynes, uses an Internet filtering system to prevent students from accessing

inappropriate web sites—and not just those that might feature sex or violence. "No football sites are allowed either," says deputy head Chris Woods.
"Otherwise the kids would just waste time." (DfES 2001, p. 13)

Elaborate measures are described and recommended for promoting and
maintaining propriety in a wider sense. "Superhighway Safety" urges "regular checks by teachers of incoming and outgoing [e-]mail [that] will reveal cases of inappropriate use" (DfES 2001, p. 5). Teachers should "often
monitor chat spaces, remotely and in person" (ibid., p. 20). It also strongly
advises schools to include automatic disclaimers at the end of each e-mail
sent by students in order to protect the school. It further suggests that
"schools may want to restrict some pupils to using internal e-mail only,
whilst providing others with greater access" (ibid., p. 5). A range of information is disseminated to teachers on a regular basis, urging caution and
the direct teaching of (social) rule-governed technology use. E-mail has
been particularly targeted in terms of safety concerns and measures.
BECTA and the DfES discuss e-mail use in terms of e-mailing "partner
schools," thereby implying a norm for practice. BECTA has also produced
a seven-page "Information Sheet on Using E-mail in Classroom Projects
at Key Stage 2" (BECTA 2001c). Besides listing what e-mail offers to
teaching and learning and offering practical application suggestions, the
sheet encourages whole-class discussion to consider "pleasures and pitfalls
of e-mail" and to establish "ground rules for e-mail use" (ibid., p. 1). These
rules, the information sheet goes on to say, should include an understanding of the following points:

- Language use in e-mail should be appropriate for a general audience.
  E-mail should be available to be read by the entire class and both
  teachers [of the partnered classes]. E-mail is not a private medium.
- Names or pen names must be included on each e-mail sent, and
  the e-mail should be addressed to a specific recipient in the partner class.
- Responsibility for who will check mailboxes should be established.
- It is necessary to decide whether e-mail should be stored electronically and where, or whether e-mail should be printed out and, if so,
  where copies should go.
- There should be sanctions if the rules are broken, and that the rules
  and sanctions are in place to protect and support people in both
  [partner] schools. (Ibid., p. 2)

The "Superhighway Safety" website provides a number of examples of
what these rules look like in practice, such as the following:

Instructions to Pupils Using E-mail
at Ambleside Primary School, Cumbria

- Ambleside Primary School in Cumbria, which was highly commended in this year's ICT in Practice Awards, provides one e-mail address for each class. Teaching staff believe this improves security, making it easier to supervise children and that the lack of individual addresses has not hindered pupils from making full use of the internet on a variety of online projects such as communicating with individual penpals from around the world, contributing to the school's award-winning website, and whole classes working with classes at schools in other countries.
- The school has developed its own set of rules to ensure the privacy and safety of pupils when using e-mail, the internet and the World Wide Web.
- These rules stipulate that children are not allowed to engage in conversation or dialogue with others on the internet without permission or supervision from their teacher. All e-mails to classes are moderated by the class teacher.
- Children are also taught never to reveal personal details, such as home addresses and telephone numbers, when they are communicating with other internet users. If they ever receive a message that makes them feel uncomfortable or upset, they are told to report it to a teacher.
- As a further precaution, downloading of files is restricted to staff (or children under supervision) and children have no access to newsgroups.
- Any other school that wishes to obtain an individual class or staff e-mail address must first contact Ambleside's ICT co-ordinator.
- Parents are encouraged to take similar precautions and invest in security software when using the internet at home with their children.
- Ambleside's internet service provider (ISP) is Schoolzone, which offers a variety of packages and security features including filtering.

Assessing the Grid

A brief descriptive overview cannot possibly convey a fully rounded picture of the Grid. Nonetheless, our sampling has been fair and representative. On the basis of what we have described we will now assess the Grid as an educational resource under three headings:

- The language of the Grid
- Counterproductivity
- Non-efficacious learning

The language of the Grid

The language of the Grid, in which its architects and developers talk of "policing," "protection," "controlling," and the like, is revealing and spells trouble for expansive educational visions. The very name "Grid" is itself illuminating. A grid is absolutely uniform. It lays down a pattern of regularly spaced horizontal and vertical lines forming squares, as used in a map as a reference for locating points. The notion of a learning grid evokes notions of regularity, uniformity, boxes, and cells, the imposition of order on a space, and the desirability of being able to fix something—or somebody—in relation to particular points or norms. This, of course, is what learning becomes like when it is mapped out as a national curriculum, with key learning stages and designated standards encoded as a system. Such a system enables regiments of functionaries to check student after student against criteria from which efficiency measures can be calculated and compared in the name of performativity (Lyotard 1984).

The National Grid for Learning is perfectly adapted to the lock-step of standards-based instruction, where "delivering learning content" becomes a pretext and a context for administrations to demonstrate fiscal accountability by showing how standards get met with ever increasing "efficiency." This involves a profound alienation of learning—a turning away of learning from authentic engagement with the world in ways that actualize human powers. Instead, learning becomes a process of wearing a path through regular and regulated points in a grid. Learning literally becomes gridlocked to the extent that teachers and learners do not actively resist alienating tendencies built into education when it is constituted as a site of performativity.

The same mindset that produced the notion of a "grid" in the first place is evident in the free and unapologetic references to "policing" and "protecting" that pepper the web pages concerned with safety and propriety on the Grid. BECTA acknowledges that a major part of its role involves "helping to police content" (NGfL 2001c, pp. 1–2). As it happens, "policing" is the right word. For example, the scope and nature of the kind of ground rules for using e-mail proposed by BECTA are draconian. They make sense only on a basis of presuming that learners have delinquent proclivities that need intense surveillance and should be subjected to random checks.

The language of recommended ground rules for e-mailing in school is precisely the language of policing, surveillance, and presumed delinquency or aberrance: "random checking," "restrictions," "rules and sanctions," "supervision," "security," and so on. Here it is worth recalling the direction indicated by the example of "excellent practice" of using filters to prevent students from accessing inappropriate sites noted above. "Inappropriate sites" quickly comes to refer not simply to sites that feature sex and/or violence, but to football sites as well.

Of course, there is more to these points about the language of the Grid than the words alone. This language, like all language, is embedded in and reflects a discursive orientation toward the world. It is born of and begets social practices—ways of doing things, ways of being, and ways of shaping what other people do and become. Here again the distinctions drawn by John Perry Barlow, which have to do with modes of controlling values, morals, knowledge, competence, and the like, are useful.

As we have seen previously, Barlow speaks specifically to the issue of pornography on the net. He does so, however, in a way that can stand in for concerns expressed on behalf of the Grid's "Superhighway Safety" about the possibility of students accessing websites involving sex and violence (and even football). Barlow rejects the imposition of gross filters designed to control access as a way of addressing the issue. They can't work because cyberspace simply cannot be controlled in that way. Barlow advocates more local, individualized filters that work on the principle of people taking responsibility for their choices and deciding what "noise" they want to filter out: "If you have concerns about your children looking at pornography the answer is not to eliminate pornography from the world, which will never happen; the answer is to raise them to find it as distasteful as you do" (quoted in Tunbridge 1995, p. 4).

Precisely the same logic can (and, we believe, should) be applied to issues and concerns like safety on the Grid. From Barlow's perspective, strategic approaches that use filters and other material forms of control (like random checking) carry over to cyberspace various models, approaches, concepts, and orientations that have evolved in physical–industrial space. This is what we see writ large in the police-and-protect operating logic on the Grid, as well as in the very concept of a Grid itself.

The particular point we want to make here begins from Barlow's suggestion that we should educate (he uses "raise") young people in ways that promote in them a strong ethical sense of what is distasteful. They then have available and can deploy the only kinds of filters that can ultimately be counted on in cyberspace. Our fear is that, contrary to this approach, the kind of protective logic used by some of the current Grid managers is much more insidious. It is symptomatic of the extent to which bureaucratized, performativity-oriented school systems have actually given up on educating and moved to other ground.

Within this mindset, what began as a desire to "protect" has become a process of conforming to practice guidelines and lists of procedures. Such is the outsider-bureaucrat's notion of enacting accountability with respect to a duty of care. But it is no guarantee of safety. To be safe people ultimately have to learn how to protect themselves—be this physically, morally, or whatever. The operating logic of the Grid impedes this process by imposing the kinds of control that try to eliminate risk, but do so at the cost of obliterating real pedagogical moments conducive to learning how to keep oneself safe in the rich sense education should be concerned with.

Counterproductivity

At numerous points the operating logic of the Grid conflicts directly with the expressed aspirations it is supposed to facilitate. Some of the typical recommendations made for policing and protecting exemplify quite specific forms of counterproductivity. For instance, the advice given on "Superhighway Safety" that schools include automatic disclaimers at the end of each e-mail message sent by students (in order to protect the school) conflicts with the emphasis found elsewhere on students learning not to identify themselves in any way in their e-mailing and online chat activities. Such seemingly small contradictions have a habit of replicating, until a system trips itself up. Hence, the suggestion on "Superhighway Safety" that schools may want to "restrict some students to using internal e-mail only, while providing others with greater access" is in tension with the government's stated aim of enhancing educational outcomes through access to ICTs. It also begs the question of who will decide, and on what criteria. The will to police and punish conflicts here with the will to enhance and encourage exploration. Such contradictions abound in the Grid.

The kind of counterproductivity that readily arises from operating a clampdown mentality around computing is evident in the example of Caleb's futile web search for information about medieval times sketched in chapter 5. The clampdown approach operating at Malveny State School contributed to a counterproductive outcome whereby Caleb concluded that looking for information on the Web is a waste of time. By turning Web searching into a tightly surveilled and artificial practice, school practice contributed to Caleb's misunderstandings about the nature of URLs, internet domains, use of search engines, and other aspects integral to effective use of the internet to locate information. Given the current constitution of the Grid, it is reasonable to expect large-scale "Caleb-like" instances to occur. Indeed, it would be unreasonable to expect otherwise. The learners most likely to be disadvantaged here are those who rely on schools for opportunities to use the internet. Those with computers at home are likely to have fewer restrictions on their access. Thus the clampdown mentality reinforces the privileges of the well-off, in contradiction to its professed commitment to equity.

The issue of counterproductivity looms large when we compare how the Grid has unfolded with the stated policy aspirations of the government. Tony Blair's (1999) observation that Britain's international competitiveness will increasingly depend on how its citizens adopt digital technologies is pertinent here. For example, by making a range of "off-the-shelf," "one-size-fits-all" resources available, the Virtual Teachers Centers may help thwart the professional development of teachers. Such canned resources suppress creativity in areas of symbolic work like designing resources in the light of conceptual and theoretical understandings embraced by teachers themselves.

The kind of competitive edge mentioned by Tony Blair has much to do with high-level symbolic-analytic work. Encouraging development of symbolic-analytic talent within school education presupposes that teachers are disposed to model such talent as often as possible. Along with the general fetish for standardized, quick-fix, packaged programs, resources, and remediation services that currently besets performativity-driven public education, the Grid works against enhancing teacher work as symbolic analysis.

Finally, with respect to counterproductivity, we should not be surprised if younger learners find little on the Grid that appeals to them or engages their attention for long. Within the small proportion of material on the Schools pages dedicated to younger learners we find a striking absence of links to resources developed by children for children. By way of contrast, an excellent counterpoint to Grid fare for young (and not so young) people is provided by a website designed and produced by Alex Balson (5 years old at the start of his project) and his father Scott (Balson and Balson 2001). *Alex's Scribbles—Koala Trouble,* is a series of 13 stories written from 1996 to 1999 about Max, the koala, and the adventures he has with his mother and friends, Joey the kangaroo, Platty the platypus, Sarah the goanna, and others.

The *Koala Trouble* stories are simple narratives requiring readers to solve problems and to "click" on image-mapped hypertext links to help Max and his friends (e.g., clicking on a tree bough to help Max back up into a tree he had fallen out of, or clicking on a stick to get Joey out of the lake). These stories were Alex's idea. As a pre-schooler and first grader he could personally find little on the web to interest him. He produced the images for his stories first by freehand, using a storyboard layout to structure narrative development. Then, with his father's assistance, he scanned them into digital format and used a graphics program to add color. He then added text, and used an HTML editor to produce the web pages. Much of the latter work was initially done by Scott. Alex did more of it as time went on.

Besides the Max stories, the website had a feedback section where children (and adults) from around the world could (and in their hundreds, did) e-mail Alex in response to the stories they had read. Another section of the website was given over to classrooms in other countries, such as Singapore and the United States, where readers "hosted" Max on his "round the world" trip. This section showcases classroom accounts, stories, and pictures describing Max's adventures in their part of the world.

The website was created to promote cooperative activity by children who are stimulated by material designed and drawn by their peers (beginning with Alex). Scott described Alex (at 5 years) as a "mean net-surfer" who found most of the material on the internet "boring." This directly stimulated the production of his own site, to meet a need he felt himself. *Koala Trouble* received 60,000 national and international "hits" in two months following its initial posting on the internet in 1996. During 1997 "*Koala Trouble* had reached an estimated audience of *1,000,000 kids of all ages* since it first went up on the internet. Today that number is closer to two million" (original emphasis; Balson and Balson 1999, p. 1). *Koala Trouble* has received numerous prestigious awards and accolades. Alex and Max continue to receive e-mail correspondence from children and adults all around the world (aged from 3 to 95 years). These are often imaginative and creative—adding episodes to Max's adventures (e.g., Max goes SCUBA diving), or relating how Max is currently with them, curled up on a bed, or hiding in bookshelves and toy bins. These e-mails not only testify to the quality of the narratives and activities on the website. They also exemplify authentic uses of e-mail as a communication medium.

Besides withholding from youngsters guided access to resources of greater inherent interest to them (like *Koala Trouble*), the Grid in its current state offers little to encourage the development of Alex-like young people. Promoting development of learners with "good understanding of ICT" and who "adopt digital technologies," in ways that will shape future cutting-edge innovations, has a lot to do with encouraging Alex-like activity now. At present the Grid constructs "good understanding of ICT" in terms of a capacity to drive the equipment safely, or with adequate protection. As Castells (2000) makes clear, however, the greatest added value associated with new ICTs involves seeing them as processes to be developed, rather than as tools or applications to be mastered at the level of use. According to Castells (2000), the information technology revolution and the emergence of a knowledge society are not so much defined by the centrality of knowledge and information—since new forms of knowledge and information are important in all such moments of major productive and developmental change—as by the way knowledge and information are applied to knowledge generation and information processing/communication devices. He refers to a "cumulative feedback loop between innovation and the uses of innovation." He notes that since the 1970s,

> the uses of telecommunications technologies have gone through three distinct stages: automation of tasks, experimentation of uses, reconfiguration of applications. In the first two stages technological innovation progressed through learning *by using* . . . In the third stage, the users learned technology *by doing* and ended up reconfiguring the networks, and finding new applications. (p. 32, emphasis in original)

Everyday diffusion of new technology amplifies its powers as it is appropriated and redefined by users through doing. This is what Castells means by identifying the new information technologies as processes to be developed as well as tools to be used. Successful new applications add economic and technological value, bestowing advantage and elite status on their inventors. This is because of the close relationship that now exists between creating and manipulating symbols (cultural activity) and the ability to produce goods and services (productive or economic activity). Within the contemporary context, then, elites learn by doing, not by using—where elites are construed as those who generate high value adds. By the same token, users can become doers "by taking control of technology, as in the case of the internet" (ibid.).

People like Alex display good understandings of ICT as "processes to be developed." This, however, is patently what the Grid in its current conception and state does *not* promote and, indeed, runs the acute risk of actively undermining.

Non-Efficacious Learning

Many limitations found in the Grid are not confined to it alone. Rather, they are instances of more general limitations we associate with conventional views and practices of school-based learning grounded in "psychologistic" models. According to these models, learning goes on in the head, and understanding and competence are primarily cognitive. Such ideas sustain the belief that learning occurs most effectively within tightly regulated classrooms, and can be designed and conducted apart from sites of embodied real-world social practices. There is a growing body of counter-evidence against the conventional wisdom about learning, and we believe a sociocultural approach to learning helps redress important imbalances (see Goodson and Mangan 1996a, 1996b; Gee 1996, 2001). From a sociocultural perspective,

> the focus of learning and education is not children, nor schools, but human lives seen as *trajectories* through multiple social practices in various social institutions. If learning is to be efficacious, then what a child or adult does *now* as a learner must be connected in meaningful and motivated ways with "mature" (insider) versions of related social practices. (Gee 1996, p. 4; emphasis in original)

Viewed from this standpoint much of what the Grid offers seems beholden to pedagogical concepts and approaches likely to generate non-efficacious learning. Once again, the "exemplary" case of Denbigh School applies here. If the view of its deputy head about blocking football sites causes concern about the degree of policing going on, it should worry us even more in relation to an ideal of efficacious learning. Not only does it appear that Mr. Woods has forgotten that the GridClubs actually include one for football; other internet football sites are among the kinds of educational stimuli that can readily support efficacious learning for large populations of learners (including many about which "inclusion" policies are supposed to be concerned).

Well-produced websites provide exemplars of mature web design and construction practices. They also offer rich possibilities for meaningful and motivated connections between what students do as learners now and insider versions of related social practices. Those practices often include leisure activities that are very important in the lives of many adults, and may involve being a valued supporter of a football club. But there are also many work-related aspects of these activities, which may range from becoming a professional football player to working in the design, marketing, and selling of football memorabilia, becoming an archivist, and so on. It could prove more difficult not to be able to turn access to a football site on the internet toward efficacious learning than to be able to. The Grid purports to facilitate lifelong learning. Yet, contradictorily, it identifies as exemplary a practice that negates the very idea of life as a trajectory, and of learning being properly concerned with building understandings of possible and viable trajectories.

The approach to e-mail taken on the "Superhighway Safety" and related sites provide further examples of infringements against principles and practices of efficacious learning. E-mail is the most widely used internet application (Shapiro and Rohde 2000, p. xviii). It may also be the one most maligned by classroom practice. Within school settings e-mailing is widely constructed as writing to penpals via the internet. To suggest e-mail should be used principally to communicate with students in another class is to miss the point of most insider uses of e-mail. E-mail use among adolescents and children is generally reported as a medium for communicating with friends and family, for sharing and accessing information such as text and music files, for participating in discussion lists, and such like. E-mail practices similar to writing to penpals are generally confined to lonely hearts and singles-in-search-of-partners internet services.

Instead of recognizing the most common real-life uses of e-mail, the rules of use promoted by BECTA and the DfES, and some practices identified as exemplars of conforming to them, distort the medium. Claiming that e-mail is not a private medium is incorrect. It is not solely or by nature a private medium. Neither, however, is it solely or by nature a public medium. Rather, e-mailing assumes numerous forms according to the social practices of e-mail users. It is no less (or more) a private medium than the telephone. Vast numbers of people use e-mailing for private purposes, including when they send messages from public facilities. It would be absurd to think Monica Lewinsky intended that the messages she sent to people detailing her trysts with the U.S. president would be made public documents (or that she would have given them freely to her work group to read). E-mail intended for general audiences is generally sent by means of the multiple recipient function, analogously to how memos or newsletters get sent to general audiences.

Similarly, such practices as providing a single e-mail address for an entire class of students and designating one person to log-on and collect the e-mail for the class seem misplaced. The latter sits uneasily with the policy aspiration that all learners master a range of information and communications technologies (BECTA 2001a, p. 1). The former, exemplified in the Ambleside School vignette supplied by DfES, is wrongheaded. This is not how institutions in the world beyond school (other, perhaps, than prisons) generally behave. Such practice contributes to preparing learners for a world that is not a world they are likely to live in. It generates distorted conceptions of social practices outside the artificial learning environment of the classroom. It would make better sense for each partner class involved in the "pen pal-ing" of e-mail to fax one another. This would at least approximate to mature versions of social practices involving fax machines. A single fax number per work unit or institutional division is normal. Moreover, the hard copy format of a fax message sent to a number serving multiple persons discourages prudent people from transmitting sensitive material that can be viewed by all and sundry.

The Grid runs serious risks of infantilizing students and teachers by feeding them key-staged websites that are often little more than master worksheets transferred to the internet. Grid fare often sells learners short by "subtracting value" from learning opportunities (our concept of subtracting value evolved in a conversation with Jay Lemke). The Owl stories described earlier are a case in point. Having been promoted as "two great stories to keep you amused" and as interactive learning opportunities, the stories renege on both offers. The story line becomes a thinly disguised excuse for narrow, basics-oriented, drill-and-skill exercises. Interactivity is essentially confined to clicking on one of two or three options, or going to the next page.

Young learners inhabit a world of burgeoning new literacies different in kind, scope, and purpose from conventional literacies and familiar language uses forged in pre-digital times (Alvermann 2002; Lankshear and Knobel 2001). The Grid does not engage with new literacies at all on the Schools pages. It does not even acknowledge them. Examples like the Owl stories do no more than provide opportunities to use a mouse, click and drag, and carry elements of conventional established language uses into electronic spaces.

This is not the stuff of a "learning society" as conceptualized in policy statements pertaining to the Grid. According to Tony Blair (1997), "children cannot be effective in tomorrow's world if they are trained in yesterday's skills." In the case of the Owl stories, as in other examples like the "interactive" @school pages, learners are being encouraged to use poorly conceptualized programs as well as to practice decontextualized literacy skills by means of yesterday's literacy drills. A learning society calls for much more sophisticated literacy understandings and learning practices than the old basics promoted in the Owl Stories and throughout Grid space generally (see Bigum 2002; Lankshear 1998; Rowan et al. 2002).

Rather than hyperlinking to appropriate online resources and referring to resources that exist in other forms than on the internet, Grid developers have tended to opt for their own purpose-built resources. This practice of re-inventing extant resources trips the Grid up in ways that impede efficacious learning, because the scale of the task interferes with the accuracy and detail of data presented. For example, the "look it up" section of the GridClub designates space for an online dictionary, thesaurus, and atlas. In one section of the atlas the map of the islands of Australia, New Zealand, and the South Pacific are labeled "Australasia." Elsewhere it is labeled "Australia and New Zealand." The clickable maps of "Australasia" allow zoomed-in views of included countries. Icons within and around each map link to corresponding information. For example, an image of shark displays a four-sentence information text pertaining to "Great White Sharks" and their presence in Australian waters. The text tacitly and falsely implies that no other kinds of sharks are found in Australian waters.

Other misleading, incorrect, or culturally insensitive information abounds. The enormous cattle and sheep stations of inner Australia are referred to erroneously as "ranches." A text on the Great Barrier Reef mentions only SCUBA diving and tourism. There is no information identifying the capital city of Australia. Flora are seemingly absent. The Aboriginal Dreaming becomes "ancient legends." This atlas is intended to be used by people seeking good quality information. Excellent alternative resources are readily available on the internet, but the Grid does not link to them. Insofar as efficacious learning presupposes access to information, the information provided should avoid error and distortion as far as possible.

Finally, we may consider an issue concerning the *Homework High* page. Offering a facility for students to post homework-related questions to be addressed by a "resident expert" is a potentially valuable resource. The value for effective learning of allowing students to post questions and requests like the majority of those we reported earlier is very dubious, however. To use the internet effectively to discover what a proscenium arch stage is, it is more appropriate to know how to go to a reputable search engine, and to learn something about conducting efficient searches in the process. What could and should a "resident expert" provide in response to requests like: "Is Philip Larkin essentially pessimistic? Help Please!!!!!!!!" or "Hi I have to write a story on Harry Potter. Can you help?" If schools cannot help students learn to ask better and more academically responsible questions they would be better staying away from the internet.

In its current and foreseeable states of development, the Grid seems likely to impede more than facilitate efficacious learning. The mindset informing its design and construction militates against its being reformed in ways likely to support expansive educational goals and to attract and sustain the interest of learners with alternative access sources to online environments. In its present and foreseeable states, the Grid is something we believe teachers and learners would be better off without.

Alternative Possibilities

The imagery of the Grid brings to mind rows of bolted-down desks, the reproduction of classroom space in cyberspace, the counterattack of an established social technology of spatial control against the new spaces being opened up by information technologies. The Grid is constrained from two directions simultaneously. First, it is tied to a mindset that sees curricular activity using ICTs as being essentially the same as learning under the regime of print. Learning simply becomes re-technologized: a matter of doing the same things as before, only with new technologies. Approaches to authority, discipline, control, and surveillance developed to deal with face-to-face situations in physical spaces are carried over to dealing with activity in virtual spaces.

Second, the Grid is itself locked into a larger grid charted by techno-cratic education policies and a performativity fetish. Elements of these factors combine to create a powerful operating logic used to shape and regulate the use of new ICTs in classroom work. The Grid cannot be re-placed by something equal to the aspirations of policy rhetoric and ex-pansive educational purposes without substantial changes occurring in the mindsets of those who shape the culture of the Grid through policy, fund-ing, site design, and implementation.

Teachers who want to use new ICTs to build rich and authentic un-derstandings of social practices mediated by the internet would do well to consider other options and approaches than those of the Grid. We will briefly mention three levels of options here.

- Locate alternative (less school-like and more intrinsically interesting) resources to those offered by the Grid. Devote less energy to creating original but crude tutorial material, and more to locating the best among the wealth of extant resources available.
- Promote approximations to real-life uses of new technologies within the context of school subject-based learning.
- Use new technologies in the context of developing the school as a knowledge provider for its local community.

We will expand upon each of these options below.

Locating Alternative Resources

Finding alternative pathways from the Grid to enable teachers and learn-ers in classrooms to benefit from information and communications tech-nology is not difficult. Contemporary educational resource publication abounds with rich, varied, high quality resources already available to teach-ers and students in digital and conventional formats. In place of the digi-tal worksheet resources offered by the Grid-endorsed @school website for, say, "physical processes" within the science subject area for Key Stage 2 (Pedagog 2001), teachers instead could easily access far superior resources like Dorling Kindersley's CD-ROM, *The Way Things Work* (Macaulay 1994; 2000) and the award-winning website, *How Stuff Works* (Brain 2000). Paper-based texts, like *The Ways Things Work* by David Macaulay (1988; 1998), which inspired the subsequent CD-ROM productions, and other beautifully illustrated, high quality, hi-tech books published especially for children (e.g., Ardley 1995; Brown 1991; Langone et al. 1999), are readily available options offering much more than the Grid.

Using books, CD-ROMs, and websites on why and how things work in conjunction with a resource like a LEGO Technic set provides rich, hands-on, and genuinely interactive classroom learning experiences. The quality, ease of use, and detail of such resources bring physical processes to life in ways that a slow-loading digital worksheet from the *@school* website simply cannot. Neither can an online cloze exercise that promotes itself by urging students to "Impress your teacher by filling in the blanks in this short article on gravity" (Pedagog 2001). The key difference is that resources like those mentioned here as alternatives to the Grid's offerings have been developed to serve genuine desires to know, rather than to fit neatly into Key Stages of the United Kingdom's National Curriculum, or to provide "busy work" activities for students.

Promoting Real-Life Uses of New Technologies

Our account of the Grid points toward two impediments to efficacious learning we believe can be addressed successfully. One is the impediment to developing hard-edged capacities to locate and evaluate information available on the internet. Activity and resource options are so regulated and confined that opportunities to develop sophisticated search practices are constrained. Moreover, because Grid-linked material has been deemed worthy by official channels and organs, incentives to subject such resources to rigorous critique are likewise limited. The second impediment is the proliferation of school-like practices that do not connect (in meaningful and motivated ways) what is learned now to mature versions of social practices.

To address these problems schools should, among other things, promote learning activities involving new ICTs that help develop the kinds of capacities advocated, for example, by Paul Gilster (1997, chap. 7). Gilster describes a practice he calls "knowledge assembly" that he regards as a necessary new literacy in and for the information age. Knowledge assembly is "all about building perspective" and proceeds through "the accretion of unexpected insights" (pp. 195, 219). Gilster describes the tools and procedures of knowledge assembly using the internet in terms of a five-step process.

The first step involves developing a customized personalized electronic news service—a personal newsfeed—by subscribing to an online news service and entering keywords that define the topics or issues you want to receive breaking stories about. The service then sends stories on topics of interest as they break (pp. 201–208).

In the second step one subscribes to online newsgroups and mailing lists that deal with the subject(s) of interest. These offer the personal viewpoints and opinions of participants on the issues in question, providing access to what (other) netizens make of the topic.

The third step is to search the internet for background information—for example, by going to the archives of online newspapers to get a history of the build-up to the story or issue thus far. Gilster also mentions using search engines to find internet links to sites covering key players in the story or issue. These may provide related stories or other information that contextualize the issue or topic, providing additional breadth, variables, and angles.

The fourth step involves drawing together other helpful internet news sources, such as online radio and oral record archives accessed by software like *RealAudio,* interactive chat sessions, video archives, and so on.

The final step in knowledge assembly goes beyond internet sources of information and involves relating information obtained from networked sources to non-networked sources like television, conventional newspapers, and library resources. This is indispensable to seeking balance and perspective. It puts the issues being addressed into a wider context of news and information, which may include prioritized contexts such as whether newspapers consistently run a story on page 1, or on page 12.

These steps involve diverse understandings, skills, and procedures. Many of these are acquired only through regular use and practice: for example, learning to find one's ways around mailing lists, news groups, and discussion lists; identifying the strengths of different search engines, and deciding which ones to use for particular areas or topics; how to narrow searches down by refining keyword checks; how to use Boolean logic in internet searches, and so on. Of crucial importance are specific tools of content evaluation that one can use along the way to filling one's information cache, item by item. According to Gilster, these tools include examining the credentials of information sources, the probable audience a source is pitched at, the likely reliability of the source, and distinctions such as those between "filtered, edited news . . . personal opinion . . . and propaganda" (ibid, p. 217).

This is not the only available approach to effective information searching and evaluating practices. It is, however, a viable option to aim for. It is a real-world practice with genuine "street cred." It is how Gilster, a highly successful journalist, writer, and critic, operates in his own work. Ideally, teachers would bolster Gilster's battery of content evaluation tools with approaches to critical appraisal of texts and the discourses in which they are embedded. They would recognize different theoretical and normative points of view and employ specialized techniques of textual and discourse analysis (e.g., Fairclough 1992; Gee 1996; McLaren and Lankshear 1994).

Real-life credibility also depends on developing approaches that recognize what students do now as learners making use of the new ICTs. Technology-related learning needs to be linked in meaningful and motivated ways to mature versions of related social practices. The ideal would be for students to learn to use ICTs in ways that genuinely approximate the uses made of them by technicians, fashion designers, journalists, historians, online consumers, participants in virtual clubs, game-playing communities, and so on. Such an approach would mean integrating use of new ICTs into a range of learning activities: collecting data, checking its quality or reliability, seeking out informed opinion relating to judgments or positions that have been advanced, participating in relevant online communities via discussion lists, locating references to works containing different points of view, and so on.

"Driving" the ICT appropriately means knowing such fundamentals as how to search, how to evaluate and follow links, and how to locate relevant sites. At the same time, and this is often what is missing in school-based academic learning, it involves using ICTs productively in a wide range of learning contexts. It means knowing how to research, explore, theorize, and solve problems in the manner of competent participants in social practices of work, domestic life, recreation, travel, and cultural pursuits. Teachers should be aware of the distinction between "pretend" or "schoolish" versions of social practices and mature versions, and they should be eager to orient teaching and learning as closely as possible toward the mature versions.

The kind of differences in question can be illustrated by the differences between two versions of "doing history." The schoolroom version conceptualizes history as a process of reading text book sources and producing written assignments. Working historians do historical work that involves checking out archives of primary source documents, building one's own archive of materials, organizing and managing data, and then analyzing them to argue for or defend a historical interpretation. The distinction corresponds to the difference between using the internet to seek answers to assignment questions or additional references to assigned textbooks, versus using the internet to locate primary source documents or information about archiving procedures, issues of historiography, and so on. Less academic variants of doing history might take in the increasingly popular practice of producing family genealogies, and the like (see also chapter 3). The same kind of reasoning can be used to project from mathematics into building, modeling, running a domestic economy, and so on.

Developing Schools as Knowledge Providers for Their Communities

In a recent discussion, Chris Bigum (2002) looks at the question of what schools might usefully do with new ICTs from an interesting perspective. He looks at some of the "design sensibilities" (Schrage 1998) that shape how new ICTs are used in schools. Design sensibilities are similar to mindsets—sensitivities or orientations that affect how we understand technologies and how we use them. Three design sensibilities that are reflected in much of the use of new technologies in schools are that ICTs are an educational good, that new technologies can be seen in terms of earlier technologies, and that the internet is about information delivery.

The first of these sensibilities encourages the "domestication" of new ICTs to pre-existing curriculum activities. Since, from this viewpoint, education equals curriculum activity, and since ICTs are an educational good, then using ICTs will help us to do better what we already do. The second is the kind of view that sees the word processor as a kind of typewriter or pencil. It encourages using computers to produce final versions of essays or projects (where rough copies have been produced in pen or pencil first). The third is associated with seeing a school web page as a medium for providing information about the school, for posting completed assignments, and so on. The extent to which we can understand the Grid in terms of such design perspectives is self-evident.

Other design sensibilities, however, may be more appropriate so far as schools are concerned. Recognizing that the biggest impact digital technologies are having and will continue to have is on relationships among people and between people and organizations, Bigum suggests an alternative design sensibility based on relationships. From this perspective, schools would consider how new ICTs might be used productively in terms of relationships that could be developed and mediated using new technologies, rather than in terms of information delivery or of doing old things in new ways. Moreover, in an age when there is a superabundance of information, the scarce resource will become point of view—a place to stand from which to deal with information and make effective use of it (Bigum 2002).

These two ideas underpin very different possibilities for what schools might do and be, and for what learning might become. Bigum explores these in terms of the school's potential relationship to its community as a knowledge provider, a space for doing full-fledged research that enhances a community's point of view. He argues that communities will increasingly need and benefit from having good quality knowledge about themselves. Such knowledge provides a local community with a sound basis for reading and responding to global and informational influences it encounters. Community self-knowledge, in other words, provides a point of view or a form of expertise from which to interpret and respond to more global forces pressing upon it. Producing, accumulating, and disseminating local knowledge will consequently become increasingly valuable to communities as they become caught up in global-level trends and processes.

Schools can have a special role to play here, since funding to develop local knowledge bases is often tagged to projects and interests framed at national and regional levels, and that are not necessarily consistent with local interests. To become knowledge providers to their communities, however, schools will have to move from the "pretend" space of current forms of curriculum-based learning, to doing investigatory work that is regarded as genuinely useful and valuable by external (community) groups. This means, once again, a move from using to doing. Instead of merely using ICTs to replicate old learning patterns, schools can move into processes of doing research that meets standards of quality, rigor, and relevance acknowledged by the community. A move in this direction, as exemplified to some extent by The Watershed project described in chapter 3, is work in which new ICTs can play an important role.

Such genuinely relevant work will go beyond the fragmentary kind of involvement schools sometimes have when students contribute to larger research projects on environment, traffic flows, and the like by collecting data such as rainfall or vehicle counts. Rather, schools will need to see research in its full sense and range of activities. They will need to build a sense of research as something they are good at and through which they can relate and contribute to their community. This is not beyond schools and students. Bigum documents the case of a primary/elementary school in a small town that has adopted an approach whereby requests made of the school for expertise or knowledge are framed in terms of the possibility of students making the response.

> On one occasion a group of local principals visited the school to inspect the approach the school was employing in its use of ICTs. While teachers structured the day and spoke on some occasions to the group, there were three workshops for principals . . . presented by students. One [workshop on] how to make claymation movies was taught by a group of [Grade] four students. The students . . . offered encouragement, advice and gave instructions without taking over or doing it for the principals. The men and women sat on the floor in their suits . . . negotiated a plot with pieces of colored plasticine and recorded over fifty images using a digital camera.

The students then taught them how to convert the stills into movie format. (Bigum 2002, pp. 7–8)

Other examples of school-community liaison were given in chapter 3. While such events in themselves may not be hugely significant, they reflect the principle of examining every opportunity for having students work on assignments that matter to the outside community (ibid.). It is a principle that entails working to understand activities of data collection, which are common enough in classrooms, beyond the limits of a "fridge door" mindset. When project work and data collection have no purpose or audience beyond the classroom, they tend to have no outcome other than as a display on a family's refrigerator door. Authentic knowledge production, on the other hand, involves moving beyond data collection to processes of assembling, analyzing, and interpreting data in terms that are relevant to community purposes and needs. It amounts to moving beyond "doing school" toward the approximation of real-world practices of consulting, contract research, and high-quality reporting.

The bottom line, however, is that the community must value the work. For this to happen "schools would have to be at least partially remade in the minds of the local community" (Bigum 2002, p. 8). Rather than a wholesale change, this could be pursued on a project-by-project basis aimed at building up "a repertoire of research skills and products" responsive to "local needs and interest" (ibid.). Building such a repertoire would in turn require discovering what kinds of research activities "can be sustained by different age cohorts," the kinds of professional support teachers would need in order to work in this way, and the kinds of strategies needed to support such new forms of school and community partnerships.

Universities are already taken seriously and engaged in such relationships. The idea is that schools may be too. The idea of schools as community knowledge resources, and the way it positions the use of new ICTs in schools, is a far cry from the underlying conceptions of the Grid. It is, furthermore, almost infinitely more educational in its vision. It embodies the principle of efficacious learning described above. And it actively resists making monkeys out of learners and ICTs alike. In this kind of context,

CCTs [computing and communications technologies] have a role in supporting and sustaining new relationships. The collection, analysis and dissemination of information is work that computers can support well. In this way, schools don't do computers for computers' sake. [They] can respond to a new communication order by reconsidering the role they play in the community. [I]t is this role . . . of knowledge production . . . that can be usefully supported by the judicious use of CCTs. (Ibid.)

Such an approach would meet National Curriculum requirements by transcending them. It is a tall order if we think in terms of how schools are currently conceived and constrained, and how such conceptions and constraints are further reinforced by institutionalized resources like the Grid. Such an approach is no more or less, however, than the kind of thing implied in Tony Blair's observation that tomorrow's needs will not be met by yesterday's skills. If we are serious about following the policy rhetoric where it leads, one of the places we will arrive at will be in schools that provide knowledge contributing to a community's point of view.

7

PARADOXES AND CULTURE CLASHES

Introduction

IN PREVIOUS CHAPTERS WE HAVE DESCRIBED, on the basis of our own research, some of the things that happen when a new social technology—in this case, the complex of new computing technologies—is imposed on the school. While the cases reported here by no means exhaust our collective research base, they are nonetheless typical of what we have seen in classrooms and virtual education spaces in the different countries in which we have worked over the past decade. Without wanting to generalize from these few studies, we believe that they will resonate with the experiences of many readers, and to this extent are indicative of larger "realities." Specifically, we see in the cases outlined here a range of quite paradoxical outcomes that appear to us to result from a form of culture clash that can be understood on multiple dimensions.

This chapter will outline several paradoxes and provide an account of why we think they arise and where the beginnings of a resolution of at least some of them might lie. It will remain an open question, however, as to whether those who have the power to redirect education in ways that might resolve some of these paradoxes—contradictions that are counterproductive so far as learning is concerned—will have the political will to do so. Rather, we think that powerful interests are served well by the paradoxical situations we describe in the pages that follow, and that for the foreseeable future learners will be living with these paradoxes and the impediments these entail for high quality learning.

By paradoxes we mean ideas that seem to be contradictory or contrary to common sense, yet appear to be plausible in the light of evidence and arguments pertaining to them. For example, "more leads to less" is a classic example of a paradox and, indeed, is one we find among the cases presented throughout this volume. Further paradoxes that arise from our cases and that will be discussed in this chapter are "greater space leads to confinement," "change produces sameness," and "the pursuit of freedom generates constraint." A key point about the kinds of paradoxes we identify in this chapter is that they span almost all of the meanings of the term. They are not simply "curious" or "odd." They are also, in some degree, "unfortunate," "less than optimal" and, even, "regrettable." We do not raise them as paradoxes simply out of intellectual curiosity or intrigue. Rather, we want to try and make their strangeness or counterintuitive character as apparent as possible in order to show how they are aberrant and in need of redress. The thing about many of the examples we see as paradoxical is, precisely, that they are so common and everyday as to appear normal: just the way things are. By identifying them as paradoxical, however, it is possible to show how and where they are strange and, more importantly, problematic when viewed from a different perspective. This is precisely what we will be trying to do with the familiar sorts of cases described in earlier chapters.

Paradox #1: More Produces Less— The Art of Subtracting Value

Paradoxically, in many instances among the cases we have reported, the addition of further technological and technology support resources actually subtracts value from learning and related purposes. This can occur in a range of ways. For example, an abundance of new technologies may result in lower quality learning than we might reasonably expect to have otherwise occurred. Alternatively, it may result in mis-learning, frustrated learning, confused learning, and so on.

Three examples may suffice here, although many others will be apparent in the cases we have outlined so far. The case of Caleb mis-learning how to locate resources on the internet is a classic instance (see chapter 4). Here we have an example of an economically advantaged school that spent untold amounts of money on state-of-the-art high-end equipment. Yet the bulk of the equipment was set up in a place that led to intense resentment on the part of the librarian, which in turn impinged directly on the conditions and the "climate" of use. Furthermore, the actual capacity of the machines was severely reduced through insistence that internet sites only be accessed statically.

Given that teachers could have accessed the internet from anywhere and downloaded sites to put on the school server, there was little or no point to even having school-based internet access. Hence, the investment in online capacities was largely wasted. Moreover, and in terms of subtracting value from learning, the way the internet was used in the school detracted from Caleb's (partial) understanding of uniform resource locators (URLs) and how they function: it contributed directly to his mis-learning that no useful resources about medieval times exist on the internet.

The point here is not only that a lot of money had been invested in a server, an intranet, and internet capacity, and that mis-learning still occurred. The point is also that teachers had been enlisted in an effort to create an artificial simulation of internet, which in turn created an artificial learning situation. They had invested time and effort in the practice of downloading and uploading material to be available as archives, which were then to be accessed in the guise of internet access. This is time and effort that could have been deployed elsewhere—particularly, given that teachers often report their current teaching experience in terms of having to do more with less.

The National Grid for Learning likewise provides numerous instances where more leads to less—to the point of actively subverting the stated purposes of particular resources. The Owl story, *Ozzie Takes a Ride,* is an example (see chapter 6). A stated aim of the story is to keep young people amused by means of a great story. The result is practically no story at all, just a set of stilted "activities" that replicate the most arid of classroom literacy exercises. Indeed, the idea that youngsters could find such engagements amusing is close to being a very scary thought. Likewise, the industry that has gone into constructing resources that convey partial and distorted representations of other countries (as in the case of the online Atlas representation of Australasia and the South Pacific) subtracts value from the labor deployed, investments made in internet connections in the home, and from potentially rich understandings of another part of the world that might more readily be promoted using existing and less resource-intensive materials.

Similar kinds of examples are evident in activities undertaken in the schools at Tipping and Danton reported in chapter 5. On the admission of the classroom teacher at Tipping, using the internet for French lessons in ways that strained bandwidth and rural phone lines beyond capacity created frequent and debilitating disruptions to classes. Equally, on the admission of the teacher at Danton, the students participating in the *HyperCard* presentation for speech night lost interest in the project and effectively had to be "guilt-tripped" into seeing it through. None of the students actually had the opportunity to learn anything significant about the very thing the teacher was initially most concerned about: namely, giving rural learners a chance to use and understand leading-edge computing applications.

It is worth considering here ways in which this paradox may be related to forms of culture clash. There are clearly elements of a clash here between assumptions and ways belonging to a culture that is outside computing space generally and cyberspace in particular, but that has nonetheless been applied directly to computer-mediated learning in schools. Computing culture aims at maximizing the potential of digital technology (Johnson 1998) and, to this extent, at fomenting new practices online and offline so far as change is required to maximize this potential. This culture puts priority on going where the digits can go: in accepting that the world is and will be different as a consequence of developing the potential of new technologies, and on taking risks and pursuing innovation that prioritize "machine beauty" (Gelernter 1999) and pursue maximum elegance between technological possibility and inventive, creative human purposes. Sometimes these purposes may be familiar ones—such as in the case of Alex's interest in telling stories appropriate to children of his age (see chapter 6). But what is distinctive about Alex's practice, and what stamps it as insider practice so far as computing culture is concerned, is that the original purpose is given over to "digital leadership." The interactive spaces opened up by Alex's stories are distinctively digital spaces—they participate in digital culture.

Outsider culture, so far as computing spaces are concerned, puts familiar practices, concerns, and operating assumptions in the saddle. It assumes that the world is essentially the same as it was previously. The only difference is that it is now technologized more intensely and in more complex ways than before. Hence, maximizing digital potential is circumscribed within bounds of familiar practice. The aim is to pursue greater efficiency rather than to embrace change. Risk management and boundary maintenance become high priorities. Established goals and purposes, concepts, issues, ways of thinking, fears, and concerns are privileged over digital capacity.

To some extent this shows up as issues of control. For example, the emphasis at Malveny was on seeking to control the limitlessness of the internet rather than exploring it. This was cast in terms of minimizing danger—construed in terms of systemic requirements developed in physical space, with respect to protecting young people from harm—rather than encouraging informed risk-taking and developing strategies for getting informed. Malveny's heavy-handed treatment of the internet had value-subtracting consequences for students like Caleb—who negotiated potentially "dangerous" internet spaces from home, with no evidence whatsoever of having yielded to temptation or of having been led astray. The triumph of outsider culture in the school had generated a low-trust environment that impeded learning potential at important points: points that are important in the sense that they refer precisely to the kinds of things today's learners increasingly have to learn how to handle.

Elsewhere, in our examples of "more producing less," outsider culture asserted itself by forcing the use of new technologies into tasks and contexts where their use was inappropriate or counterproductive, but which conformed to school ways of doing things. We heard this tendency spoken of when teachers guiltily related their concern that they hadn't yet found a way to incorporate computers into their practice. We observed it when the internet was used to obtain graphics in real time for foreign-language lessons, even though download speeds could not coincide with the audio feed coming via telephone. Such a practice is simply a bad option that regularly had disruptive effects within the remote electronic classrooms we observed. It presupposed a teacher-centered pedagogy that was heavy on bandwidth and where the technology could not cope. Educators working from inside a computing culture would have looked for ways to use the new technologies to support learning on terms more in tune with their capacities and local conditions.

In the case of maximizing teachable moments within *Ozzie Takes a Ride,* the issue is perhaps less one of culture clash than "culture trash." It makes little difference to the quality of children's learning experiences whether cats and dogs hitting shuttlecocks bearing the words "happy" and "unhappy" and faces depicting smiles and frowns are presented as pages in a book, sequences in a television show, or slide show–like sequences on the internet. Such resources insult learners of whatever age or level. The fact that they exist in other media does not mean that we should accept them within new media. Very young insiders, like Alex, are acutely aware of this. Professional educators and IT consultants should be taking their lead from cultural insiders, rather than projecting such timeworn inanities into new media. The fact that this is being done on the back of large budgets derived from taxes on wage and salary earners adds insult to injury.

Paradox #2:
Increased Space Leads to Confinement

A second paradox, which is especially evident in the case of the National Grid for Learning, involves the manner in which the emergence of practically "limitless" information space on the internet results in learners being subjected to intense confinement and surveillance with respect to their information accessing practices.

As we have seen, mechanisms of confinement go as far as using tracking software with which teachers can actually spy on student internet use.

Other mechanisms include the euphemistically named "walled gardens"—paid services that metaphorically build walls around "safe" sites and shut them off from sites that are deemed not safe for users to view. Unfortunately, the "Superhighway Safety" site associated with the Grid does not provide criteria for how to distinguish safe content from that which is not safe. If we take the Grid-approved sites as ostensive definitions of "safe," it is clear that the Grid errs on the side of bland rather than risky; cute rather than challenging, mature, or hard-edged; and "faux-interactive" (with interactivity confined to clicking on items to move around the website) rather than full-fledged forms of interactivity that involve people (or people and software programs) "acting on each other."

Full-fledged interactivity is exemplified by a game like *Majestic* (Electronic Arts 2001) that involves participants in winning or "solving" the game by means of accessing websites, sending faxes and e-mails, receiving phones calls and e-mails, chatting with others about game play, and the like. This is the kind of full blown interactivity that justifies the label "interactive." Interactivity is a crucial element of *Majestic*—take it away and there is no game (unlike *Ozzie Takes a Ride,* where the so-called interactivity could easily be automated with no change whatsoever to the story). The interactivity in episodic games like *Majestic* (or *Banja, The Cypher,* and the like) requires players to learn how to solve complex problems using complex media of communication and information, and, needless to say, it becomes a logical model for learning more generally when seen from the standpoint of computer-culture insiders.

It seems that the Grid's concern to make the internet safe for students has been taken by schools to signal an open season on constraining student access to internet-based information and informational exchanges. Seemingly, the more extensive information space becomes, the more learners are subjected to constraints against their freedom to search out, transmit, and even produce information. The more divergent and rich the variety of information potentially available on the internet becomes, the more the creators of the Grid narrow down what is actually available to learners on Grid-approved websites. In the end, this is confined to thinly disguised National Curriculum content, with interactivity largely reduced to clicking on icons or buttons allowing learners to move to other parts of the website offering more of the same.

Paradoxically, the more intense and pervasive official rhetoric becomes about the power and potential of the internet as a key resource in developing "learning" or "knowledge" societies, the more education-related new technology enterprises and practices appear to be committed to shutting down possibilities for students to learn how to become effective citizens in a learning society. This paradox can be seen in terms of clashes between insider and outsider cultures occurring along several dimensions.

First, the paradox can partly be seen in terms of the entrenchment of an outsider culture in what Bezos calls "first phase automation" thinking, as opposed to the kind of commitment to "second phase automation" characteristic of insider computing culture. Cases like the Grid and most of the school sites we have described are involved in using the new technologies simply to "do the same old . . . processes, but just faster and more efficiently" (Bezos, quoted in Spector 2000, p. 16). Indeed, it is questionable whether the "faster and more efficiently" applies, but "the same old processes" certainly does. Being committed to "doing the same process you've always done" projects the use of digital technologies into familiar terrain of authority, discipline, and constraint.

Classrooms are quintessential modernist spaces of enclosure (Lankshear, Peters, and Knobel 1996). They have always operated according to spatial, temporal, and normative logics of confinement. Disciplining bodies has always been integral to the work of schools (Foucault 1977). The current sociocultural-technological conjuncture presents an opportunity to approach learning in terms of "second phase automation." To do so would be to "fundamentally change the underlying . . . process and do things in a completely new way" (Spector 2000, p. 16). It would call for taking some risks, engaging in some genuine interactivity, and trying to invent curriculum and pedagogy to some extent on the fly. This is what is *not* happening in most of the cases described in earlier chapters. Hence, the potentially vast spaces that have emerged with new communications and information technologies and within which and through which learning might occur are being made over into familiar spaces of confinement.

Second, the tendency toward confinement exemplifies Barlow's account of the difference between insider and outsider mindsets in terms of understanding cyberspace in spatial terms, and how issues are addressed in light of these understandings. As we outlined in chapters 4 and 6, Barlow addresses the issue of safety on the internet in terms of pornography. He contrasts an outsider mindset, which thinks in terms of the kinds of strategies of control employed in physical space, with the kinds of approach taken by insiders, who conceive of cyberspace in non-physical terms. Hence, the recourse to filters, firewalls, downloaded websites archived on a server to displace time online, the use of tracking software and the like all betray the physicalist mindset of outsiders.

Resolving the paradox by which enlarged space leads to confinement presupposes willingness to move toward a mindset that takes a less paternalistic-protectionist approach to the duty of care. This would, instead, endeavor to tackle safety on the internet in more educative ways that aim at developing self-regulation on the part of users, in accordance with criteria and principles they acknowledge as binding on ethical and prudential grounds.

Such an approach involves a measure of risk, and it is certainly a more challenging road to follow than gross filtering and other forms of heavy-handed policing. In the end, however, the latter will become increasingly less effective as more people spend more time on the internet, and as the internet increasingly displaces conventional resources within formal educational settings. Now is the time to start thinking about the alternatives and educating teachers to consider them.

Third, the tendency toward practices that generate confinement out of enlarged space is a consequence of a particular kind of spatial imagination that emphasizes systems over networks. Sarah Whatmore and Lorraine Thorne (1997) talk about two very different ways that people think about the phenomenon popularly referred to as "globalization." One approach views globalization as a process whereby huge systems, that are "always already constituted" (e.g., global commodity systems, transnational corporate and financial systems, a rejigged global capitalist system spearheaded by supernational organizations like the World Bank and OECD), "engage in a colonization of surfaces which, like a spreading ink stain, progressively colors every spot on the map" (p. 287).

The other way is to think of institutions that have global reach is as networks that achieve their global reach by becoming "longer," more stable, and robust. Global networks are performative orderings that are always in the making. They stand or fall on the efforts of those involved in them ("actors") to increase and consolidate the length and durability of networks that are hybrids made up of people, devices, codes, and other living and nonliving things, which enable "acting at a distance" (ibid.). Whatmore and Thorne, drawing on Actor Network Theory, argue that systemic approaches to understanding, explaining, and responding to globalization involve a "failure of social and spatial imagination" (ibid.). Instead, they advocate understanding globalization in terms of the creation, consolidation, and growing of actor networks that are "woven of the same substances as . . . more humble everyday forms of social life" typically regarded as local (ibid., p. 288).

With a little manipulation, the kind of distinction drawn by Whatmore and Thorne between systems and networks as competing analytical metaphors (ibid., p. 288) can provide an angle for thinking about policies and practices around computing that produce confinement out of enlarged space. Where learning is thought of in terms of systems already in place, that have established and binding procedures and requirements, and the like, it is natural to transfer what is seen as faits accomplis over to developments like incorporating new ICTs into school-based learning. This results in attempts to develop blanket approaches to concepts like "internet safety" that can be systematized, turned into checklists, and recommended practices, against which schools can be deemed accountable in relation to concepts like "duty of care." But safety and protection, like learning itself, are not, and cannot be, ensured by systems. Rather, they are produced, consolidated, and maintained by networks that enact and make robust the kinds of practices, relationships, and values that promote conditions like "being safe" and "coming to learn."

Although the language of computing has been saturated with talk of "systems," insiders to the new generation of computing are much more at home with talk and procedures that emphasize networks and networking (cf. Castells 1996). The same trend is evident in the rhetoric of learning, although much less so in the actual practices of learning within formal sites. We believe that adopting the new spatial imagery advocated by Whatmore and Thorne provides a key not merely to welcoming and harnessing the enlarged potential learning spaces enabled by new digital technologies in ways that resist confinement, but also to reconceptualizing learning in forms that will be necessary for successful participation in any "knowledge society" worthy of the name.

Paradox #3: Change Leads to Sameness, the Future Points to the Past

The cases we have described provide plenty of instances of the tendency within schools to maintain their established ways—those that have become sedimented—in the face of technological change. With very few exceptions, the teacher life-history and observational data obtained in the Ontario schools reported in chapter 2 exemplify a process of change leading to the perpetuation of sameness. The teachers reported their efforts to find ways of making the computer fit in with their styles of teaching, with whole class approaches, and so on. The data pointed strongly to the probability that introducing computers had not and would not substantially change the ways that the teachers involved in the study would conduct their lessons and approach classroom learning. As one teacher commented, "I don't think I've had to do too many things differently because of it."

Such attitudes reflect a long-standing response to imposed innovations, voiced by another teacher's framing of the challenge in terms of the ques-

tion, "How can I do what I have always been doing in a new context?"
Even within the "road to Damascus" experience of the reluctant adopter,
Jim, the evidence is that when he began using the computers he was using
them to do work he would otherwise do by different means (e.g., photo-
copying maps from a hardcopy atlas, rather than printing them out from
the internet). This complemented the approach of the design teacher,
which was to use *CAD-Tutor* software to replace something from the existing curriculum with something the computer could be used to do.

Precisely the same was evident, albeit with small differences in detail,
in each of the sites explored in the remote rural region in Australia. In
one school we see a class trying to use the internet to obtain information for a project about space, as an alternative to using print-based resources, and in a second classroom the students were similarly using a
CD-ROM encyclopedia and e-mail to gather information to be used in
a project on the environment that would otherwise have been obtained
from printed materials. In this second case a student argued the advantages of the CD-ROM source over conventional books in terms of two
kinds of efficiencies. One was that the digital source would be more up-
to-date. The other was that the students could print directly from the
CD-ROM data, which would save them having to copy the material for
presentation.

At another site within the same study the situation was essentially the
same, albeit in an extra-curricular context. The teacher began from a desire to give students a chance to learn how to use new technologies and
found a brief window of opportunity at the end of the year, centered on
augmenting the principal's end-of-year speech. Here, then, we have a further example of a new technology being incorporated into an established
routine and being used in the way that technology from an earlier era (e.g.,
a conventional slide projector coupled to an audio source, or using a conventional camera to photograph aspects of the school and school life)
would previously have been used. At the same time, students enacted familiar extracurricular roles (doing odd jobs to help out), and participated
in a longstanding logic of work: namely, the division of labor into separate
tasks, directed by the teacher. The future points emphatically to the past in
this example.

The paradox of change leading to the same and the future pointing to
the past intimates a looming culture clash. It can be seen as a form of outsider computing culture, nurtured within the extant directions and priorities of the school as a regulatory technology, colliding with the potential
for movement to an insider position, which would incorporate more open
and free-form learning.

Two aspects of this clash seem important to us. The first is that once again, in the schools we observed, we see cases of first-phase automation being enacted within classrooms. Participants are involved in the same processes as previously, but with a sense that it is more efficient, or somehow more appropriate, to use new technologies in place of older ones. There is no conception—no mindset—that the new technologies represent a challenge to "doing learning" in radically different ways, along the lines that would be involved in the active exploration, experimentation, and innovation inherent in second-phase automation.

So far as official rhetoric about the role of education being to prepare learners for the knowledge society is concerned, the irony is that it is second-phase automation and not first-phase automation that defines the knowledge society. This is the point made emphatically by Manuel Castells, as reported in chapter 1. Of course, this is by no means a paradox at the level of school and classroom operations. It is writ large in policy-driven initiatives like the Grid, which, as we have seen, is a clumsy and heavy-handed exercise in restricting rather than opening up cyberspace for students, in doing the same old business by different means.

The second aspect of culture clash involved in the paradoxes of change leading to sameness, and the future pointing to the past, pertains to the inability of educators to conceive of new and authentic learning purposes to which new technologies might be put. That inability results in outcomes like the speech-night slide presentation being the best that could be made of a bad overall situation. It occurs because teachers, as much as policy makers, education administrators, curriculum developers, and the like, often have not had much experience with using new technologies for their own real-life purposes. In many cases they have not participated in online communities involved in innovative developments, or had opportunities to reflect on how such practices and their innovative dimensions are relevant to school-based learning—in terms of what it may be useful to learn, and in terms of how learning occurs when one is on the inside of computing culture learning communities.

This paradox, like the others, will only be resolved as and when schools, school administrations, and education policy makers move from understanding the educational potential of new technologies in terms of first-phase automation, systems, and physical space to insider-like understandings. At present this does not represent a culture clash within education to the extent that currently there is no insider computing culture evident within education at the level of policy development and leadership. Such as it exists, the clash is between computer-mediated learning culture inside schools and computer-mediated learning culture within insider spaces, such as online communities, innovative practice communities, and so on. There is, however, a very important dimension of culture clash that is especially relevant in terms of this third paradox. This concerns the clash between the outsider culture represented in school appropriations of new technologies and the presence of "insiders" within the student population of our schools. It is possible that many students have insider understandings that point toward the future in ways that school practices do not, and whose sensitivities are offended, undermined, confused, or otherwise compromised or negated by what they experience in the way of computer-mediated learning in school.

The cases we have presented have not explored the nature and extent of insider sensitivities among students. By the same token there are indications, as with the example involving Caleb, of students whose insider experiences of internet practices and communities have been contravened by school practices, with counterproductive outcomes. These are no more than indications, but they point to possibilities that beg further investigation. Some researchers (e.g., Green and Bigum 1993) have long entertained the possibility that teachers may be aliens in their own classrooms from the standpoint of student understandings of and involvement in digital technology cultures. Numerous books have explored facets of youth technological savvy in depth, and in ways that suggest that many students pointed more directly toward the future will be experiencing serious cultural clashes between their insider sensitivities and school-based uses of new ICTs.

This in itself is paradoxical. Students with insider sensitivities provide potential keys for resolving paradoxes like "more produces less," "increased space leads to confinement," and "change leads to the same." Yet, in cases like the Grid and the practices implemented in schools like Malveny, we find policy makers, education administrators, and teachers alike actively undermining the chances of resolving such paradoxes by imposing—wittingly or unwittingly—on youthful insiders thoroughly outsider perspectives and ways.

Paradox #4:
Freedom Generates Constraint

We have found repeatedly in our research that the potential for various kinds of enlarged personal and social freedoms regularly associated with the internet and mature computer use (i.e., by adults for work-related and entertainment purposes)—and dating back even to the birth of the internet under the funding of the U.S. Defense Department, but with remarkable autonomy in terms of project development and use (see Hafner and Lyon 1996)—have often materialized in practice as new forms of constraint impinging on students, teachers, and schools. We have already discussed how the abundance of information on the internet has repeatedly led to strategies that diminish the internet for students in the name of safety and "duty of care." In this section, we focus on the effects of the open, unmoderated spaces of a particular new technology innovation for schools when they run up against a series of sedimented systems.

The Watershed project discussed in chapter 3 is a good example of freedom generating constraint. Here again, Whatmore and Thorne's distinction between system and network is useful. It provides a way of explaining in the context of The Watershed how carefully conceived teacher and school autonomy in relation to a formal new technology project actually became a constraining force in the lives of participating schools. The project can readily be seen as an innovative network that ran up against the long-established systems of the education bureaucracy and of local commercial business.

The network was meant to involve schools, local communities, and local businesses in mutually beneficial relationships. Students would produce archives of local history and geography information that could be accessed and added to by community members. In the process, they would learn how to make good use of database software, Geographical Information Systems, and the like. The developers intended that local businesses would provide financial support to fund the project within each school, and receive "free" publicity in return. Unfortunately, at the time of the introduction of The Watershed project into schools, there had been a change in provincial government that strongly impacted on existing regimes of practice. New legislation and policies demanded more from teachers, not only in terms of actual teaching hours, but also in terms of their "duty of care" toward students, and in coming to grips with mandated new curricula in every subject area (introduced more or less simultaneously).

The network aspirations of the developers of The Watershed project began to unravel more or less as soon as schools agreed to participate. First, the project seemed to receive the warmest welcome in schools serving small towns, which unfortunately put the onus for funding onto small businesses in the area—many of whom were struggling to balance their books each month as it was. Moreover, larger companies did not seem all that interested in participating as funders. Notwithstanding Ministry of Education rhetoric that partnerships between schools and businesses were a good thing, the system of business operating in the province was not geared toward becoming a node within a network that was as distributed and, in many ways, ephemeral as The Watershed project.

A further clash between system and network in the case of The Watershed project came about via the sheer sophistication and size of the software architecture for The Watershed program. This system had particular, unchangeable requirements (e.g., disk drive space, graphics programs) that far outstripped the technology present in participating schools (and in the homes of teachers, as well). None of the schools in The Watershed network were in a position to help each other out technology-wise, either. Besides, teachers had little time for networking in relation to the project anyway, because the sophisticated software needed all of their spare time and attention to master, even at a basic level. Thus, in many cases, The Watershed program itself was never fully operationalized or used to its full potential in schools.

The developers deliberately built numerous freedoms into The Watershed (such as freedom from Ministry funding and curriculum mandates, unfettered limits to data base sizes constructed by students). Yet, it seems that the size and scope of the envisaged Watershed project actually confined the project to the small number of schools that had invested heavily in it in terms of computers and teacher time. These schools have been left, in the end, flogging a dying horse with little real freedom to unhitch the saddle and walk away.

In many ways, it could be said that without appropriate supports in place—or situated networks of co-participants, existing hardware and software, financial investors, and the like (cf. Whatmore and Thorne 1997, p. 288)—the ethos of freedom associated with the internet is compromised not only by schools' moves to control and contain student access, but also by the clash of networks and systems, by tensions between funding and autonomy, and idealized concepts of freedom in the face of operational realities for schools.

Paradox #5:
Enlarged Freedom Leads to Greater Discipline

To this point the paradoxes we have identified have been cast as less-than-optimal outcomes of clashes between cultures: as things to be resolved. Moreover, we have framed the cultures in tension in a somewhat binary manner: insider tending to carry positive connotations and outsider tending to carry more pejorative connotations. This approach has the usual limitations and runs the usual risks of employing binaries. We accept these risks because we think it is important to get such issues and ways of thinking about them on the table. While the cultural range we have worked with is polarized and underdeveloped, we believe it is sufficient to provide a basis for further exploration of cases such as those we have presented, and for beginning to think of ways to make principled progress around the imposition of a new social technology on the established social technology that is the school.

To complete our discussion we want to introduce briefly a new case from which we derive a paradox that goes in the opposite direction from those we have presented so far. This case comes from a second site in the same project on which the account of Malveny State School (see chapter 5; also Bigum et al. 2001) was based. This was a project originally designed to explore possibilities for counteracting disadvantage in literacy education. Drawing on ideas informed by Barlow's account of opposing mindsets around new technologies, the research team framed and enacted projects involving the use of new ICTs that departed from conventional classroom approaches in three main ways:

- The teaching and learning group in each of the four sites was to be a cluster comprised of a teacher, a teacher in training, one or more cultural workers from the community, and four to six students deemed one way or another to be "disadvantaged."
- Learning sessions were to take place outside of school hours and outside the designated curriculum, although on school sites.
- The learning activity was to consist of a project that would be conceptualized and undertaken collaboratively within the cluster, and would be completed in 20 hours of face-to-face activity over a semester (with as much work done between sessions as participants were motivated to do).

Since clusters were structured to maximize the chances of a mix of outsider and insider mindsets, the projects would ideally involve processes of negotiating across mindsets, from scratch, to come up with tasks to which all participants were committed, and to which all felt they could contribute, and from which all felt they could learn.

In the Yanga Headlands site the teacher participant was the English coordinator, Lucy (who was also deputy principal). She invited four 14-year-old male students (all Grade 9s) to participate. Their teachers regarded all these students as "trouble" and as having big problems with literacy. The boys themselves concurred in these appraisals. In interviews and conversation they gave numerous examples of their disruptive behavior in class. With respect to literacy, and classroom learning generally, they expressed negative opinions of their own abilities at the start of the project. Stuart, for example, regarded himself as being about Grade 6 level in most things at school, and openly declared that he hated writing. The other three shared that sentiment. Ben described himself as a "fast forgetter," and at the start of the project feared he would not be able to remember the processes involved in creating web pages. Even so, at that same time Stuart described how he could strip his motorcycle and reassemble it in working order, and told us that when he gets stuck he simply "reads the manual."

None of the boys was attending their regular daily English class as a result of being "too disruptive." Instead, they were studying with Lucy and working on projects that focused on things they were interested in. They had recently worked on producing a magazine based on their shared interest in motorcycles. Lucy had suggested these boys be the student participants in the project, and they had agreed. The other members of the cluster (including Lucy, when her time permitted; two academics who had played key roles in conceptualizing the project; a student teacher; and a research assistant) provided an open and supportive collegial environment. Not surprisingly, the group decided to collaborate on building a website about motorcycles. Only one member of the group (an academic) had previous expertise with web page construction.

Over the duration of the project the students mastered the basic concepts and tools of web page design and construction. The same students had previously been dismissed from a keyboarding class where they misbehaved out of boredom at being required to, as they put it, just "tap, tap, tap" at keys. They has also been barred from using the school computers to access the internet for breaking the rules that were a condition for obtaining their "license" to use the internet. (The school had instigated this system of licenses to regulate student internet use in response to fears about pornography, issues associated with school duty of care and accountability requirements, and so on.) Nonetheless, by the time the project had run its course, all four boys agreed unreservedly to serve as peer tutors to teach what they had learned to their classmates in regular class lessons, and even strategized a way for doing this that would match availability of computers during scheduled class time.

Interestingly, evidence emerged incidentally during the sessions of sophisticated literate capacities and literacy-related knowledge that the four boys possessed: evidence that belied their reputations as "literacy challenged" learners. Unprompted, they showed sound and unexpected appreciations of copyright regulations. One student (Kyle) provided a highly articulate account of the importance of context in writing. Asked if he could help translate a note left by Lucy to inform the group of something (but which failed to communicate its intent), Kyle critiqued the note on the grounds that it lacked sufficient detail and, using a concrete example, compared this to notes his mother sometimes wrote him that similarly failed to achieve their purpose.

While only one of the boys (Stuart) had previously spent much time navigating the internet, all four showed a good awareness of the function of the internet and its relationship to everyday social practices. Jarrod, for example, knew that web pages needed to be fast-loading in order to "hold people's attention." He made this comment in the context of advising the others not to put too many pictures onto each page. He grasped what matters on the internet, where speed is everything (Johnson 1998) and attention is the goal (Goldhaber 1997).

Finally, this study reminded us that schools have always traded on their claimed capacity to provide students with the literacy skills that are required for contemporary living. Schools argue that they are best placed to teach students about where and how to give their attention to what is worth knowing. However, schools at present do not necessarily teach or even promote the literacy skills and understandings that students need right now in their lives. Moreover, schools seem currently to lack the kind of mindsets and economics of attention needed to gain and sustain the real—as opposed to illusory (Goldhaber 1997)—attention of many students in literacy education (see Bigum et al. 2001, chap. 5). One result of this is the continuing exclusion, failing, and negative labeling of students who, in fact, have more than ample literacy to negotiate the spaces in which they will spend much of their time. More problematically, the kind of irrelevance and associated exclusion characteristic of so much school education effectively locks many students out of the kinds of opportunities that would permit them to learn what they need for negotiating other spaces in which they could well want to participate and excel, given the option.

It seems to us that the case of Yanga Headlands raises an interesting and positively productive paradox that can be captured in the idea of enlarged freedom leading to greater discipline. One obvious way of reading this example is that four male adolescents who had been excluded from class on the grounds of persistent misconduct (which they freely admitted to), who were labeled as "trouble-makers," as boys with literacy problems who struggle to learn in class (and who saw themselves as poor learners), responded to a more open and free learning context with highly disciplined, responsible conduct and considerable achievement. They were ready and willing to go back to class and serve as peer tutors in the aspects of web page design and construction they had acquired—despite early protestations that they would do nothing of the sort.

Of course, a single instance proves nothing or, at least, proves very little. There were many favorable factors operating in this example, including the small class size. By the same token, the data collected at this site includes information—much of it unsolicited and otherwise undirected—that points toward insider understandings and interests of the boys that simply were not engaged within routine classroom learning. They volunteered that their misconduct in the computing class was associated with the "tap, tap, tap at keys" approach.

In a similar way, Jarrod's awareness of the need for fast-loading web pages, and the boy's general familiarity with the role of the internet in everyday practices, suggest they would be well-placed to take up and be challenged by learning approaches that reflect procedures, protocols, and principles associated with insider computing cultures. Indeed, their commonalities extended beyond insider computing cultures. Their shared interest in motorcycles was an obvious galvanizing component, which points toward the role and significance of affinity groups in the lives of contemporary youth (Gee 2001).

Whatever the reasons and whatever the degree to which this kind of example might be generalized or transferred to similar contexts, it is clear that a pedagogical approach designed from the standpoint of Barlow's account of an insider mindset worked well at Yanga Headlands—as, indeed, it ultimately did within the highly constrained setting at Malveny.

In reviewing these paradoxes, one important lesson is that as existing patterns of social discipline and social boundaries break down, partly as a result of the new socio-technological order, a response has been to desperately try and reassert discipline in the social space of schooling. So, at the macro level, there is the breakdown of boundaries between the school and the outside world, particularly the virtual world that new technologies produce. Hence, many of the identity projects that school students are involved in are developed with passion and purpose outside the school, in external communities, and in the new virtual communities based in new technologies.

Against this bourgeoning insider culture, the schools themselves have, in a variety of ways, begun to micro-manage the social space of schooling in ways that were unimaginable a few years ago. This micro-management takes many forms: the self-management of the finances of each school, hiring decisions, and the like, as well as the micro-definition of the curriculum and tests that students have to take. It is as if the loss of control at one level is being responded to by a reassertion of the most minute control efforts at another.

Some of our paradoxes (and others identified in the literature we have reviewed) turn on the potential of new technologies to transform the practices and procedures of schooling. Clearly, as computer technology is introduced into schoolwork, teachers' lives and work are potentially transformed. One response has been a growing defense of existing teacher routines and teacher working practices, and a specific defense—often in passionate form, as evidenced in a number of the vignettes in this book—of existing teachers' subject subcultures. Here we have the potential liberations and loosenings that go with the introduction of new technology being set against an increasing defense of teachers' habitués at the micro-level.

In a more general sense, the potential of technology to loosen certain modes or sedimentations of social discipline and social hierarchy is countered by an increasing dependence on the use of face-to-face strategies of social reproduction in the school and classroom. It is as if the social order requires face-to-face material subjectivity to be embodied in this personal confrontation in the school at a time when looser regimes of social processing are being promoted by the new technological order. It seems that at the point of social reproduction, the social order is unwilling to embrace the possible liberations and flexibilities of the new technological world. In general, what this means is that we are facing a broad transformation of social life and social work by the introduction of new technologies; but this is faced on the other side by a growing minimization and micro-management of the social spaces and routines of schooling. At this point, it is unclear how this culture clash will be resolved, or how this growing dichotomization might be dissolved.

The dimensions of culture clash may go even deeper. Some teachers, like those whose activities are described in chapters 4 and 5, and some ICT developers like the group described in chapter 3, have found that ICTs can open up new spaces for experimentation and exciting new applications. In some jurisdictions, however, the authorities have (consciously or unconsciously) sensed that cyber spaces are spaces over which they must reassert their control. In the case of the United Kingdom's National Grid for Learning, this impetus is crystal clear.

But it is not only governments that are attempting to reassert their control of culturally influential spaces. In the last decade, we have seen other social spaces that might have contained potentially liberatory room to move—such as popular music, film, and the graphic arts—consolidated under the control of some of the largest multinational corporations in the world. In a similar way, and despite the inherent difficulties in controlling systems such as the internet, emerging cyber spaces are being enclosed by the regimes of global capital as well as their supportive state governments, in order to insure that only the limited creativity required by entrepreneurs is allowed to flourish.

In such jurisdictions ICTs are promoted, but only in the service of training and retraining, only in areas that reinforce the mobility and docility of the global labor supply. Through a series of legislative and administrative measures, projects lying outside the priorities of the dominant institutions have been starved, undermined, or simply squeezed out of the picture by the escalating demands for accountability, increased productivity, and closer conformance with centralized policy.

Historically, capital has shown an impressive capacity to co-opt and incorporate virtually every potentially threatening counter-movement. But if the trends described above lead to growing polarization, the ongoing accommodation process may not be sustainable. Time will tell, but in the interim we do have some options. This volume has attempted to identify some of those options, and to encourage our readers to envision others through a reconsideration of the culture clashes taking place as the social spaces and emerging cyber spaces of education collide.

APPENDIX

STATISTICAL ANALYSIS OF CLASSROOM INTERACTION

Table 1 Mean Proportion of Instructional Time Devoted to Various Activities, by Classroom Type

Classroom Type	Type of Activity		
	Teacher-Initiated	Teacher Questioning	Small Group
Regular classroom	0.367	0.095	0.508
Regular and computer class	0.153	0.108	0.754
Computer classroom	0.190	0.033	0.789
Computer laboratory	0.120	0.019	0.907
Overall	0.277	0.073	0.644
F ratio	4.627	3.080	4.233
Degrees of freedom	3;41	3;41	3;41
Significance of F	0.007[*]	0.038[*]	0.011[*]

Notes: [*]Significant at the 0.05 level.

1. Figures are based on classroom observation of activities, standardized to represent the proportion of the total time observed devoted to each type of activity.

2. Classrooms were classified according to their level of computer use. A "regular classroom" involved no computer use; a "computer classroom" involved use of computers in the normal classroom for the full period observed; "regular and computer class" was a mix of these two arrangements. "Computer laboratory" involved the class going to a different room with a local-area network of computers.

3. These data were originally reported in the *British Education Research Journal* (Goodson and Mangan, 1995b).

Table 2 Summary of Results from Two-Way Analyses of Variance on Proportion of Instructional Time, by Discipline and Classroom Type for Each of Three Activities

| | Type of Activity | | |
Source of Variance	Teacher-Initiated	Teacher Questioning	Small Group
Discipline			
F ratio	2.28	6.80	15.00
Degrees of freedom	2;41	2;41	2;41
Significance of F	0.100	0.003[*]	0.000[*]
Classroom type			
F ratio	4.62	4.60	8.65
Degrees of freedom	3;40	3;40	3;40
Significance of F	0.009[*]	0.009[*]	0.000[*]
Two-way interaction			
F ratio	0.55	0.29	1.52
Degrees of freedom	6;40	6;40	6;40
Significance of F	0.770	0.936	0.205[*]

Notes: [*] Significant at the 0.01 level.

1. Figures are based on classroom observation of activities, standardized to represent the proportion of the total time observed devoted to each type of activity.

2. Classrooms were classified according to their level of computer use described in note 2 to table 1. In addition, they were broken out according to three "disciplines" representing subject subcultures: social sciences, family studies/technological studies, and art. For more complete discussion, see Goodson and Mangan, 1995b.

3. These data were originally reported in the *British Education Research Journal* (Goodson and Mangan, 1995b).

REFERENCES

AAUW (American Association of University Women). 2000. "Tech-Savvy: Educating Girls in the New Computer Age." http://www.aauw.org/ 2000/techsavvybd.html. Accessed June 20, 2000.

Adams, Dennis, and Mary Hamm. 1996. *Cooperative Learning: Critical Thinking and Collaboration Across the Curriculum.* 2nd ed. Springfield, Illinois: Charles C. Thomas.

Adler, Richard. 1997. *The Future of Advertising: New Approaches to the Attention Economy.* Washington, D.C.: The Aspen Institute.

Alvermann, Donna E., ed. 2002. *Adolescents and Literacies in a Digital World.* New York: Peter Lang.

Ardley, Neil. 1995. *How Things Work: 100 Ways Parents and Kids Can Share the Secrets of Technology.* London: Reader's Digest.

Ashton, Catherine. 2002. "Foreword by the Minister for Early Years and School Standards." http://safety.ngfl. gov.uk/ schools/ document. php3? D=d40. Accessed July 20, 2002.

Balson, Alex, and Scott Balson. 2001. Alex's Scribbles: Koala Trouble. http://www.scribbles.com.au/max/about.html. Accessed August 13, 2001.

Bangert-Drowns, R. L., J. A. Kulik, and C-L. C. Kulik. 1985. "Effectiveness of Computer-Based Education in Secondary Schools." *Journal of Computer-Based Instruction* 12: 243–256.

Barlow, John Perry. 2000. "The Economy of Ideas: Selling Wine Without Bottles on the Global Net." http://www.eff.org/~barlow/Economy-OfIdeas.html. Accessed April 25, 2001.

Becker, Henry J., and Nira Hativa. 1994. "History, Theory and Research Concerning Integrated Learning Systems." *International Journal of Educational Research* 21 (1): 5–24.

BECTA (British Educational Communications and Technology Agency). 1999. "Connecting Schools, Networking People 2000." http:// vtc.ngfl.gov.uk/uploads/text/csnp_complete–29674.pdf. Accessed July 26, 2001.

————. 2001a. "Building the Grid: Aims of the NGfL." http://www.becta.org.uk/buildingthegrid/ngflaims.html. Accessed July 26, 2001.

————. 2001b. "Information Sheet on the National Grid for Learning." http://www.becta.org.uk/technology/infosheets/pdf/ngfl.pdf. Accessed May 11, 2001.

————. 2001c. "Information Sheet on Using E-mail in Classroom Projects at Key Stage 2." http://www.becta.org.uk/technology/infosheets/pdf/e-mailks2.pdf. Accessed May 11, 2001.

Bell, Daniel. 1973. *The Coming of Post Industrial Society.* New York: Basic Books.

Ben-David, Joseph, and Randall Collins. 1966. "Social Factors in the Origins of a New Science: The Case of Psychology." *American Sociological Review* 31 (4): 451–465.

BESA (British Educational Suppliers Association). 2000. Press Release: "Teachers and Computers: Competent and Confident." http://www.besanet.org.uk/news/ict2000.htm. Accessed August 11, 2001.

Bigum, Chris. 2002. "Design Sensibilities, Schools, and the New Computing and Communications Technologies." In *Silicon Literacies,* edited by I. Snyder. London: Falmer-Routledge.

Bigum, Chris, Leonie Rowan, Michele Knobel, Colin Lankshear, and Michael Doneman. 2001. *Confronting Disadvantage in Literacy Education: New Technologies, Classroom Pedagogy, and Networks of Practice.* Queensland, Australia: Project for the National Language and Literacy Institute child/ESL node.

Blair, Anthony. 1997. "Connecting the Learning Society: The Government's Consultation Paper on the National Grid for Learning." http://www.dfee.gov.uk/grid/consult. Accessed July 26, 2001.

————. 1999. "Foreword: National Grid for Learning: Open for Learning, Open for Business. The Government's National Grid for Learning Challenge." http://www.dfee.gov.uk/grid/challenge/foreword.htm. Accessed May 3, 2000.

Bolt, David, and Ray Crawford. 2000. *Digital Divide: Computers and Our Children's Future.* New York: TV Books.

Bork, Alfred M. 1985. *Personal Computers for Education.* New York: Harper & Row.

Bradford Council. 2001. "Bradford Community Grid." http://www.bradford.gov.uk. Accessed July 26, 2001.

Brain, Marshall.l 2000. "How Stuff Works." http://www.howstuffworks.com. Accessed September 11, 2000.

Brown, David. 1991. *Eyewitness Visual Dictionaries: Everyday Things.* London: DK Publishing.

Bucher, Robert, and Anselm Strauss. 1976. "Professions in Process." In *The Process of Schooling: A Sociological Reader,* edited by M. Hammersley and P. Woods. London: Routledge and Kegan Paul.

Carlson, Elizabeth. 1991. "Teaching with Technology: 'It's Just a Tool.'" Paper presented at the annual meetings of the American Educational Research Association, Chicago.

Castells, Manuel, ed. 2000. *The Rise of the Network Society.* Oxford: Blackwell.

Clinton, William. 1994. *Goals 2000, Educate America Act.* Washington, D.C.: Department of Education.

———. 1996. State of the Union Address. http://www.law.ou.edu/hist/state96.html. Accessed May 31, 2002.

———. 1997. State of the Union Address. http://www.law.ou.edu/hist/state97.html. Accessed May 31, 2002.

Cole, Susan G. 1990. "The Piper Plots a Scheme to Destream." *Education Forum* 16: 19–22.

Cooper, Margaret, and Dianne Temby. 2000. "Mindsets: The Sticks and Stones that Break More than Bones." http://www.wwda.org.au/mindset.htm. Accessed June 11, 2001.

Cummins, Jim, and Dennis Sayers. 1995. *Brave New Schools: Challenging Cultural Illiteracy through Global Learning Networks.* New York: St. Martin's Press.

DEQ (Department of Education Queensland). 1994. *English in Years 1 to 10 Queensland Syllabus Materials: English Syllabus for Years 1 to 10.* Brisbane: Department of Education.

———. 1995a. *The Computers in Learning Policy.* Brisbane: Department of Education.

———. 1995b. *Guidelines for the Use of Computers in Learning.* Brisbane: Department of Education.

DfES (Department for Education and Skills). 2001. "Making the Internet safe. Superhighway Safety." http://safety.ngfl.gov.uk/?S=2. Accessed August 11, 2001.

Dublin, Max. 1989. *Futurehype: The Tyranny of Prophecy.* Markham, Ont.: Penguin.

Dyer-Witheford, Nick. 1999. *Cyber-Marx: Cycles and Circuits of Struggle in High-technology Capitalism.* Urbana: University of Illinois Press.

Electronic Arts. 2001. "Majestic." http://www.ea.com/worlds/games/pw_majstc00/hatted_jump_page.jsp. Accessed October 8, 2001.

Fairclough, Norman. 1992. *Critical Language Awareness.* Harlow: Longman.

Foucault, Michel. 1977. *Discipline and Punish: The Birth of the Prison.* London: Allen Lane Penguin.

———. 1980. "Questions on Geography." In *Power/Knowledge: Selected Interviews and Other Writings 1972–1977,* edited by M. Focault. Brighton: Haverster.

Fullan, Michael, M. B. Miles, and S. E. Anderson. 1988. *Strategies for Implementing Microcomputers in Schools: the Ontario Case.* Toronto: Ontario Ministry of Education.

Fullan, Michael, and Suzanne M. Stiegelbauer. 1991. *The New Meaning of Educational Change.* 2nd ed. New York: Teachers' College Press.

Funk-Unrau, Neil. 1999. Review of *The Mindsets Factor in Ethnic Conflict,* by Glen Fisher. http://members.aol.com/peacejnl/revfish.htm. Accessed June 11, 2001.

Gee, John P. 1996. *Social Linguistics and Literacies: Ideology in Discourses.* London: Falmer.

———. 2001. "Reading as a Situated Practice: A Sociocognitive Perspective." *Journal of Adolescent and Adult Literacy* 44 (8): 714–725.

Gee, John P., G. Hull, and Colin Lankshear. 1996. *The New Work Order: Behind the Language of the New Capitalism.* Boulder, CO: Westview Press.

Gelernter, David. 1999. *Machine Beauty: Elegance and the Heart of Technology.* New York: Basic Books (Reprint Edition).

Giddens, Anthony. 1993. *Modernity and Self-Identity: Self and Society in the Late Modern Age.* Stanford: Stanford University Press.

Gilster, Paul. 1997. *Digital Literacy.* New York: John Wiley and Sons.

Giroux, Henry. 1995. *Channel Surfing.* New York: Routledge.

Goldbard, Arlene, and Don Adams. 1978. *Comprehensive Cultural Policy for the State of California.* Sacramento: California Arts Council.

Goldhaber, Martin. 1997. "The Attention Economy and the Net." http://firstmonday.dk/issues/issue2_4/goldhaber. Accessed June 2, 2000.

Goodson, Ivor F. 1980. *Curricular Conflict 1895–1975.* Ph.D. Thesis, University of Sussex.

———. 1992a. *School Subjects and Curriculum Change* (revised 3rd ed.). Philadelphia: Falmer.

———. 1992b. *Studying Teachers' Lives.* New York: Teachers' College Press.

———. 1995. *The Making of Curriculum: Collected Essays* (2nd ed.). London and Washington, D.C.: Falmer.

———. 2001. "Social Histories of Educational Change." *Journal of Educational Change* 2 (1): 45–63.

———, ed. 1985. *Social Histories of the Secondary Curriculum: Subjects for Study.* Philadelphia: Falmer.

Goodson, Ivor F., and J. Marshall Mangan. 1992. "Computers in Schools As Symbolic and Ideological Action: The Genealogy of the ICON." *The Curriculum Journal* 3 (3): 261–276.

———. 1995a. "Developing a Collaborative Research Strategy with Teachers for the Study of Classroom Computing." *Journal of Information Technology for Teacher Education* 4(3): 269–287.

———. 1995b. "Subject Cultures and the Introduction of Classroom Computers." *British Educational Research Journal* 21 (5): 613–628.

———. 1996a. "Computer Literacy as Ideology." *British Journal of Sociology of Education* 17 (1): 65–80.

———. 1996b. "Exploring Alternative Perspectives in Educational Research." *Interchange* 27 (1): 41–59.

———, eds. 1991a. *Qualitative Educational Research Studies: Methodologies in Transition*. Vol. 1, *RUCCUS Occasional Papers*. London, Ontario: The University of Western Ontario.

———, eds. 1991b. *Computers, Classrooms, and Culture: Studies in the Use of Computers for Classroom Learning*. Vol. 2, *RUCCUS Occasional Papers*. London, Ontario: The University of Western Ontario

———. eds. 1992. *History, Context, and Qualitative Methods in the Study of Education*. Vol. 3, *RUCCUS Occasional Papers*. London, Ontario: The University of Western Ontario.

Goodson, Ivor F., J. Marshall Mangan, and Valerie A. Rhea, eds. 1991. *"Curriculum and Context in the Use of Computers for Classroom Learning": Summative Report from the Project*. London, Ontario: University of Western Ontario.

Green, Bill, and Chris Bigum. 1993. "Aliens in the Classroom." *Australian Journal of Education* 37: 119–141.

GridClub. 2001a. "Grown Ups." http://www.gridclub.com/grown_ups/index.shtml. Accessed August 11, 2001.

———. 2001b. "Join the clubs." http://www.gridclub.com/join_the_clubs/index.shtml. Accessed August 11, 2001.

Grosvenor, Ian, Martin Lawn, and Kate Rousmaniere. 2000. "Imaging Past Schooling: The Necessity for Montage." http://www.greenhill.wyenet.co.uk/Leuven%20Workshop%201998. Accessed December 4, 2001.

Hafner, Katie, and Matthew Lyon. 1996. *Where Wizards Stay Up Late: The Origins of the Internet*. New York: Touchstone.

Harasim, Linda. 1995. *Learning Networks: A Field Guide to Teaching and Learning Online*. Cambridge, MA: MIT Press.

Haughey, Margaret. 2000. "Pan-Canadian Research Options: New Information Technologies and Learning." In *A Pan-Canadian Research*

Agenda, edited by Y. Lenoir, W. Hunter, D. Hodgkinson, P. de Broucker, and A. Dolbec. Ottawa: Canadian Society for the Study of Education.

Heller, Nelson, et al. 2001. "UK Government Stays the Course with NgfL." *Heller Report on Educational Technology Markets,* February 12.

Hirst, Paul Heywood. 1983. *Educational Theory and Its Foundation Disciplines.* London; Boston: Routledge & Kegan Paul.

Hodas, Steven. 1993. "Technology Refusal and the Organizational Culture of Schools." *Educational Policy Analysis Archives* 1 (10).

Homework High. 2001. "Homework High." http://www.home-workhigh.com/. Accessed August 11, 2001.

Institute for Cultural Democracy. 1998. "Webster's World of Cultural Democracy." http://www.wwcd.org/policy/index.html. Accessed August 11, 2001.

Johnson, Steven. 1998. *Interface Culture: How New Technology Transforms the Way we Create and Communicate.* New York: HarperEdge.

Knapp, Linda, and Allen D. Glenn. 1996. *Restructuring Schools with Technology.* Toronto: Allyn & Bacon.

Knobel, Michele. 1999. *Everyday Literacies: Social Practice, Students, and Discourse.* New York: Peter Lang.

Koschmann, Timothy, ed. 1996. *CSCL: Theory and Practice of an Emerging Paradigm.* Edited by G. M. Olson, J. S. Olson, and B. Curtis. Mahwah, NJ: Lawrence Erlbaum.

Labaree, David F. 1997. "Public Goods, Private Goods: The American Struggle Over Educational Goals." *American Educational Research Journal* 34 (1): 39–81.

Langone, John, Samek Peter, Andy Christie, and Bryan Christie. 1999. *National Geographic's How Things Work: Everyday Technology Explained.* New York: National Geographic Society.

Lanham, Richard. 1994. "The Economics of Attention." Paper presented at 124th Annual Meeting, Association of Research Libraries.

Lankshear, Colin. 1998. "Frameworks and Workframes: Evaluating Literacy Policy." *Unicorn* 24 (2): 43–58.

———, ed. 1997. *Changing literacies.* Buckingham, England: Open University Press.

Lankshear, Colin, and Chris Bigum. 2000. "Literacies and New Technologies in School Settings." *Curriculum Studies* 7 (3).

Lankshear, Colin, Chris Bigum, Cal Durrant, Bill Green, Eileen Honan, Wendy Morgan, Joy Murray, Ilana Snyder, and Martin Wild. 1997. *Digital Rhetorics: Literacies and Technologies in Education Current Practices and Future Directions* (3 volumes and Executive Summary). Canberra: Department of Employment, Education, Training and Youth Affairs.

Lankshear, Colin, and Michele Knobel. 2001. "What is 'Digital Epistemologies'?" http://www.edca.cqu.edu.au/~de/what.html. Accessed July 26, 2001.

Lankshear, Colin, Michael Peters, and Michele Knobel. 1996. "Critical Pedagogy and Cyberspace." In *Counternarratives: Cultural Studies and Critical Pedagogies in Postmodern Spaces,* edited by H. A. Giroux, C. Lankshear, P. McLaren and M. Peters. New York: Routledge.

Lankshear, Colin, Ilana Snyder, and Bill Green. 2000. *Teachers and Technoliteracy: Managing Literacy, Technology and Learning in Schools.* St. Leonards, NSW: Allen & Unwin.

Lebaron, John, and Catherine Collier, eds. 2001. *Technology in its Place: Successful Technology Infusion in Schools.* San Francisco: Jossey-Bass.

Levinson, Eliot. 1990. "Will Technology Transform Education or Will the Schools Co-opt Technology?" *Phi Delta Kappan* 72 (2): 121–126.

Liao, Yuen-Kuang. 1992. "Effects of Computer-Assisted Instruction on Cognitive Outcomes: A Meta-Analysis." *Journal of Research on Computing in Education* 24 (3): 367–380.

Lyotard, Jean-Francois. 1984. *The Postmodern Condition: A Report on Knowledge.* Minneapolis: University of Minnesota Press.

Macaulay, David. 1988. *The Way Things Work.* London: Dorling Kindersley.

———. 1994. *The Way Things Work.* London: Dorling Kindersley.

———. 1998. *The New Way Things Work.* London: Dorling Kindersley Multimedia.

———, 2000. *The Way Things Work 2.0.* London. Dorling Kindersley Multimedia.

Maddux, Cleborne, D. LaMont Johnson, and Jerry Willis. 2001. *Educational computing: Learning with Tomorrow's Technologies.* 3rd ed. Boston; London: Allyn and Bacon.

Mangan, J. Marshall. 1994. "The Politics of Educational Computing in Ontario." In *Sociology of Education in Canada,* edited by L. Erwin and D. MacLennan. Toronto: Copp Clark Longman.

———. 1998. "'The Watershed': New Technologies Supporting New Forms of Education." In *Proceedings of the World Conference on Educational Multimedia, Hypermedia & Telecommunications. Freiburg, Germany 1822–1824.*

McLaren, Peter, and Colin Lankshear, eds. 1994. *Politics of Liberation: Paths from Freire.* New York: Routledge.

Meadows, Donna. 1999. "Two Mindsets: Two Visions of Sustainable Agriculture." http://www.enn.com/enn-features-archive/1999/08/080699/donatella_4795.asp. Accessed June 11, 2001.

Merriam, Sharan. 1997. *Qualitative Research and Case Study Applications in Education.* San Francisco: Jossey-Bass.

Moll, Marita, ed. 2001. *But It's Only a Tool! The Politics of Technology and Education Reform.* Ottawa: Canadian Centre for Policy Alternatives.

MWK. 2000a. "MWK: Social-Cultural Animation." http://www.mwk16.com. Accessed May 24, 2002.

———. 2000b. "Justin." http://www.mwk16.com/perfectstrangers GRUV/vvalley/mis/justin.htm. Accessed December 10, 2001.

———. 2000c. "Virtual Valley: Brunswick & beyond . . ." http://www.mwk16.com/perfectstrangers/GRUV/vvalley/phase2.htm. Accessed December 10, 2001

Negroponte, Nicholas. 1995. *Being Digital.* New York: Vintage.

NGfL (National Grid for Learning). 2002a. "Community Grids." http://www.ngfl.gov.uk/comgrids. Accessed July 26, 2002.

———. 2002b. "Jobs." http://www.ngfl.gov.uk/jobs/index.html. Accessed September 7, 2002.

———. 2002c. "National Grid for Learning." http://www.ngfl.gov.uk. Accessed July 26, 2002.

———. 2002d. "School." http://www.ngfl.gov.uk/schools/. Accessed July 26, 2002.

Noble, Douglas D. 1991. *The Human Arsenal.* Philadelphia: Falmer.

Ontario Ministry of Education and Training. 1995. *The Common Curriculum: Policies and Outcomes, Grades 1–9.* Toronto: Queen's Printer for Ontario.

———. 1998. *The Ontario Curriculum: Social Studies and Humanities, Grades 9–10.* Toronto: Ontario Ministry of Education and Training.

———. 1999. *Choices into Action.* Toronto: Ontario Ministry of Education and Training.

Ontario. Royal Commission on Learning. 1995. *For the Love of Learning: Report of the Royal Commission on Learning.* Toronto: Queen's Printer for Ontario.

OTA (Office of Technology Assessment). 1988. *Power On! New Tools for Teaching and Learning.* Washington, D.C.: Government Printing Office.

———. 1995. *Teachers and Technology: Making the Connection.* Washington, D.C.: Government Printing Office.

Oz New Media. 2001. "Ozzie Takes a Ride. Act 1." http://www.gridclub.com/have_a_go/english/owl3book1/book01/yr3/book01/webstory/bk01storyact01.htm. Accessed August 11, 2001.

Pedagog. 2001. "@school." http://www.atschool.com. Accessed September 3, 2001.

Perelman, Lewis J. 1992. *School's Out.* New York: Avon Books.

Peters, Laurence. 2000. "Bridging the New Digital Divide: Lessons from Across the Atlantic." *Technos: Quarterly for Education and Technology.* 9 (2): 26.

Point of View. 2000. "Current Teacher's Resources." http:// academy.pointofview.cc/teacher_resource_CP.htm. Accessed January 10, 2000.

Pollock-Ellwand, Nancy. 1998. *Blair Cultural Landscape Inventory Project: Final Assessment.* Toronto, Ontario: Ontario Ministry of Citizenship, Culture, and Recreation.

Reid, William A. 1992. *The Pursuit of Curriculum: Schooling and the Public Interest.* Edited by A. Woodward and I. Westbury. Norwood, NJ: Ablex.

———. 1999. *Curriculum as Institution and Practice: Essays in the Deliberative Tradition.* Mahwah, NJ: L. Erlbaum Associates.

Robertson, Heather-jane. 1998. *No More Teachers, No More Books: The Commercialization of Canada's Schools.* Toronto: McClelland & Stewart.

Rose, Ellen. 2000. *Hyper Texts: The Language and Culture of Educational Computing.* London, Ontario: Althouse Press.

Rossman, G. B., H. D. Corbett, and W. A. Firestone. 1988. *Change and Effectiveness in Schools: A Cultural Perspective.* Albany, NY: SUNY Press.

Roszak, Theodore. 1986. *The Cult of Information.* New York: Pantheon.

Rowan, Leonie, Michele Knobel, Chris Bigum, and Colin Lankshear. 2002. *Boys, Literacies and Schooling: The Dangerous Territories of Gender Based Literacy Reform.* Buckingham: Open University Press.

Rushkoff, Douglas. 1995. *Cyberia: Life in the Trenches of Hyperspace.* San Francisco: Harper Collins.

———. 1996. *Playing the Future: How Kids' Culture Can Teach Us to Survive in an Age of Chaos.* New York. Harper Collins.

Scardamalia, Marlene, and Carl Bereiter. 1996. "Computer Support for Knowledge-Building Communities." In *CSCL: Theory and Practice of an Emerging Paradigm,* edited by T. Koschmann. Mahwah, NJ: Lawrence Erlbaum.

Schrage, Michael. 1998. "Technology, Silver Bullets and Big Lies: Musings on the Information Age." http://www.educause.edu/pub/ er/review/reviewArticles/33132.html. Accessed January 26, 2000.

Schwab, Joseph, Ian Westbury, and Neil J. Wilkof. 1978. *Science, Curriculum, and Liberal Education: Selected Essays.* Chicago: University of Chicago Press.

Schwier, Richard A., and Earl R. Misanchuk. 1993. *Interactive Multimedia Instruction.* Englewood Cliffs, NJ: Educational Technology Publications.

Shapiro, R., and G. Rohde. 2000. *Executive Summary. Falling Through the Net: Toward Digital Inclusion.* Washington, D.C.: U.S. Department of Commerce, Economic Statistics Administration, and the National Telecommunications and Information Administration.

Sheffield Council. 2001. "Citinet." http://www.citinet.org.uk. Accessed July 26, 2001.

Smaller, Harry. 1998. "Internal and External Politics: Teachers' Unions and the Struggle to Defeat Bill 160." Paper presented at Joint Session at the Annual Meetings of the Canadian Society for Studies in Education and Canadian Sociology and Anthropology Association, Ottawa, Ontario.

Spector, Robert. 2000. *Amazon.com: Get Big Fast.* New York: HarperBusiness.

Tapscott, Dan. 1998. *Growing Up Digital: The Rise of the Net Generation.* New York: McGraw-Hill.

Tunbridge, Nat. 1995. "The Cyberspace Cowboy." *Australian Personal Computer,* 2–4.

Ulmer, Gregory. 1987. "The Object of Post-criticism." In *Postmodern Culture,* edited by H. Foster. London: Pluto Press.

Wakefield Council. 2001. "Wakefield Internet Learning Domain." http://www.gowild.org.uk. Accessed August 12, 2001.

Whatmore, Sarah, and Lorraine Thorne. 1997. *Nourishing Networks: Alternative Geographies of Food.* London: Routledge.

Wills, Michael. 2001. "Foreword. Superhighway Safety." http://safety.ngfl. gov.uk/document.php3. Accessed August 11, 2001.

Winters, Kevin. 1996. *America's Technology Literacy Challenge.* Washington, D.C.: U.S. Department of Education, Office of the Undersecretary.

Yin, Robert. 1994. *Case Study Research: Design and Methods.* 2nd ed. Newbury Park, CA: Sage.

INDEX